Y0-BRO-677

What Happens in Library Filing?

by

Herbert H. Hoffman

Linnet Books 1976

Library of Congress Cataloging in Publication Data

Hoffman, Herbert H
  What happens in library filing?

    Includes index.
    1. Alphabeting.   2. American Library Association. Sub-
committee on the ALA Rules for Filing Catalog Cards. ALA
rules for filing catalog cards.   I. Title.
Z695.95.H6   025.3′7   75-28187
ISBN 0-208-01557-4

© 1976 by Herbert H. Hoffman
First published 1976 as a Linnet Book
an imprint of The Shoe String Press, Inc.,
Hamden, Connecticut

Printed in the United States of America

Dedicated to Rita, my love,
and Cheryl, my pride.

Contents

Acknowledgements

This book owes its existence to many motivational forces. Foremost among these are some people to whom credit should be given. They are Rolland E. Boepple, Director of Library Services, Santa Ana College, who in a sense caused it all by placing me in charge of the catalog, and who sparred with me on words and similar items and made many valuable suggestions; Alice Price and May Dunning, Library Technicians, who shared many puzzles and frustrations of practical filing with me, prompting me to look more carefully into the rules; and the many students entrusted to my care who unwittingly tested my ideas during the ordeal of studying the *ALA Rules for Filing Catalog Cards*, a book that is hard to understand, with a teacher who seemed even more so.

Introduction

For an activity that is so widely practised in all libraries, the filing of cards into a card catalog is based on a strikingly meager body of clearly stated principles. The *ALA Rules for Filing Catalog Cards*,* probably the most widely used and the most often cited filing manual in the field, presents more than three hundred different, detailed rules of filing practice on 235 pages of text. There is no telling how many woman hours of earnest effort the seven members of the Subcommittee on the A L A Rules for Filing Catalog Cards contributed. Before the work was finally ready for publication in the Summer of 1968, editor Pauline A. Seeley had spent years gathering information on the filing practices of hundreds of libraries. Yet this impressive body of specific rules is, in the end, nothing more than could be expected from a team of librarians trained to solve problems by data collection rather than analysis: a rich collection of traditions supported by only three very brief paragraphs on general principles that occupy less than a full page.

The following chapters are an attempt to trace and record the principles behind the *ALA Rules,* and to provide a step-by-step guideline to the decisions a competent filer must make, and in what order. It is hoped that filers and aspiring filers will thereby gain a better perspective of the system and

---

*ALA Rules for Filing Catalog Cards. 2nd ed. Edited by Pauline A. Seely. Chicago: American Library Association, 1968. Hereafter referred to as ALA Rules.

that this will help them to study, absorb, and apply the rules with greater efficiency and less frustration.

To illustrate what I mean by frustration, let us look critically at the first of the basic rules presented on page 2 of the *ALA Rules*. Let us put the short and simple Rule 1.B to the test. Figure 1 illustrates five hypothetical catalog cards:

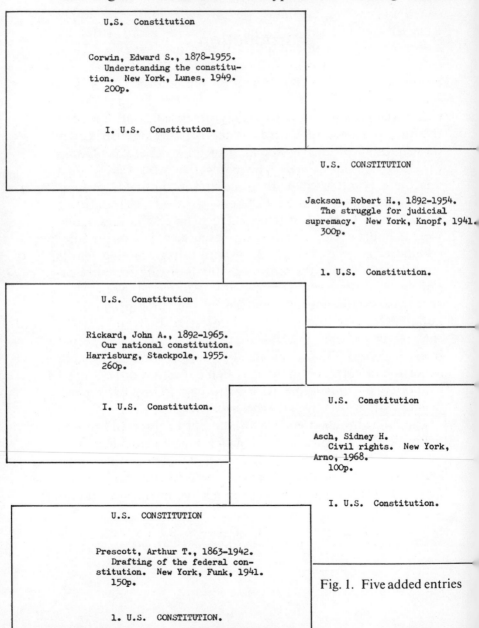

Fig. 1. Five added entries

Heeding the admonition given under "Basic Principle" that "filing should be straightforward" (*ALA Rules*, p.1); taking note of the last paragraph under "Explanatory notes on the text", according to which we pay no attention to typography, treating capitals and lower case letters alike (*ALA Rules*, p.xii); and disregarding kind of entry as directed under "Basic Order" (*ALA Rules*, p.1), we apply Rule 1.B and file these five cards word by word, letter by letter. We begin with the first word on the first line ("U."), then go to the next word ("S."), and so on. We find that up to and including the third word ("Constitution") these five cards are alike. It is the letter that follows "Constitution" that varies on all five cards, and on the basis of this difference (A<C<J<P<R) we file the five cards in the order shown in figure 2.

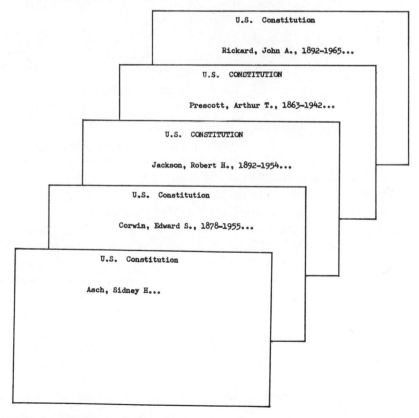

Fig. 2. Five added entries filed by Rule 1.B.   9

Yet although we followed the rules to the letter we have misfiled our five cards! We should have turned to Rule 31.C which reveals that different kinds of entries under the same geographical name heading such as "U.S." are separated into groups before filing. This actually contradicts an earlier rule, 19.A.2, which specified that entries are "arranged word by word, disregarding kind of entry". As it turns out, kind of entry makes a lot of difference in filing. Rules 31.C.1) and 2) spell this out for us: "U.S. Constitution" (as heading of an author entry) files ahead of "U.S. CONSTITUTION" (as heading of a subject entry). In other words, our five cards are filed according to the example given on page 168 of the *ALA Rules*:

"U.S. Bureau of Education
U.S. Constitution
U.S. CONSTITUTION
U.S. Office of Education"

We put all the author entries in one group, and all the subject entries in the second group. Figure 3 gives the five cards in final order.

What makes filing by the *ALA Rules* particularly frustrating in real life situations is the fact that often no proper directions are given. Nowhere does it say in Rule 1.B, for example, that one must also use Rule 31.C. There is no hint under Basic Order on page 1 that we must sometimes consider a third ordering principle (Author before Subject), in addition to alphabetical and numerical order. Many rules are imprecise: now we file item by item, now word by word, with never a definition of either term. Quite a few rules contain contradictions: in the introductory note to Rule 5 we are told that an abbreviation is a word shortened by any method. Yet the very first type of word included under this rule is the single letter, which by no stretch of the imagination can be called a shortened word. Many rules are extremely convoluted: we are told in Rules 1.B and 4.A that every word is regarded, *except* initial articles; *except* in certain proper names; *except* compounded initial articles;

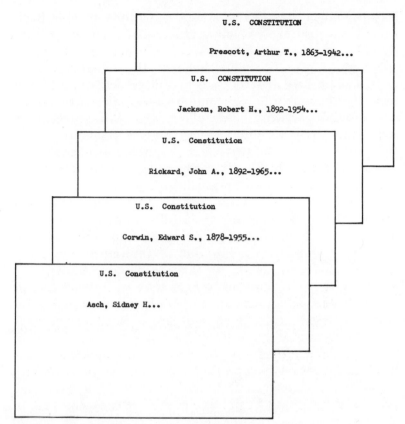

Fig. 3. Five added entries filed by Rule 31.C.

except Dutch "'s". And some of the rules raise serious questions about the candor of their compilers: there is nothing under Basic Principle on page 1 that would lead us to suspect that the "few situations" where the principle is not applied include all of the following Rules that say "disregard" or "file as if . . ." (i.e. disregard, transpose, or mentally insert something):

2.D.1	6.E	10.A	17.A	25.A.2	26.B.9.a(2)
2.D.2	7.A	11.A.1	20.A.3	25.A.3	27.C.1
2.D.3	8.A	14.A	20.A.5	25.A.4	31.F
4.A.1	8.B.1	14.B	20.E.6	26.B.2	36.C.4
6.A.1	8.E	14.F	22.A	26.B.6	36.E.1
6.D	9.A	15.A.1	23.A.1	26.B.9.a	36.E.5
					37.D.2

11

If thirty-seven specifically stated violations of the Basic Principle constitute "a few" situations, what allowances should one make for the rest of the book?

Yet absurd as all this may seem to us, our intellect tells us that filing *is* an orderly, well organized activity; that it is logically impossible to file catalog cards unless we apply a set of definite criteria and follow a regular sequence of steps. Intuitively we know, then, that in filing we follow strict rules in order to arrive at a prescribed arrangement of cards. Thousands of library card catalogs attest to the fact that this is actually accomplished.

But if it is essential to traditional manual filing that those making the decisions understand fully what is *really* done when a card is filed, how much more important will this understanding be for the librarian of the future! For automation is likely to remain on the agenda. And as the profession's brief and inconclusive encounter with the electronic computer has demonstrated, automatic data processing for libraries must be considered a dream until librarians have critically examined every last detail of every single one of their rules and procedures, and have firmly understood the theoretical concepts behind them. This is true for all library applications, of course. But it is particularly true for the automatic ordering of catalog entries. We have the best of reasons, therefore, to find out what happens in library filing.

Part I

1. Basic Principle

According to the dictionary, filing is the process of arranging papers in a methodical manner. In our narrow context we can say that it is the process of arranging catalog cards, cross-reference cards, and guide cards. The resulting set of methodically arranged cards is what constitutes a card catalog or a card file.

When we speak of catalog cards we visualize pieces of thin cardboard 7.5 x 12.5 cm in size. Although it is true that most books can be described on one such card, this is not true for all books. A certain proportion requires two or more cards to hold the full description. Any such decklet of cards, in many catalogs tied together with string, that serves to represent one bibliographic unit is treated in filing as one card. To avoid confusion between a card proper (a single piece of cardboard) and a decklet of cards treated as a unit, the term "entry" has come into use. Since in filing we are not concerned with individual cards but with entries, the term entry will be used throughout these pages in the sense of the *A.L.A. Glossary of Library Terms**: "a record of a book in a catalog".

With these definitions in mind we can describe filing as the process of placing entries into a card file in such a way that a certain prescribed arrangement results. That "pre-

*_A.L.A. Glossary of Library Terms_, prepared by Elizabeth H. Thompson. Chicago, ALA, 1943.

scribed arrangement", of course, is what all filing manuals attempt to codify. In most American libraries today, filers rely on the *ALA Rules* for this purpose. However, as we have seen, the approach to the *ALA Rules* is not as easy and direct as would be desirable. It is entirely fitting for us, therefore, to make it our first task to uncover the basic principle of filing catalog cards, the one basic distinguishable ingredient that imparts to the operation of filing catalog cards its characteristic qualities.

Is there such a basic principle? Is there one characteristic, one general rule that is true for every single filing operation, without exception? The answer is, yes. Let us consider a hypothetical entry:

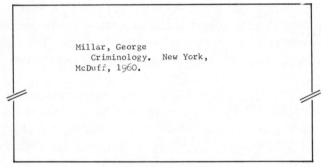

Fig. 4. Main entry

Let us pretend we wanted to file this entry into the miniature catalog pictured here:

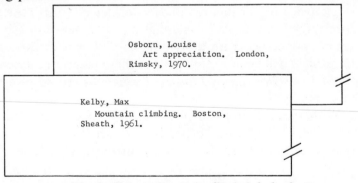

Fig. 5. Two main entries filed alphabetically

16

Since the catalog is what we "aim" at, we might call the catalog the "target file". The entries that are already located in the target file, then, are "target entries". In the example, "Kelby . . ." and "Osborn . . ." are target entries. The entry we wish to file can be called "source entry". In the example, "Millar . . ." is the source entry.

We find that the source entry (Millar . . .) outranks the first target entry (Kelby . . .), but is outranked by the second target entry (Osborn . . .). Therefore, the source entry files between the two target entries shown. Here is a picture of the target file after the source entry has been inserted in its proper place:

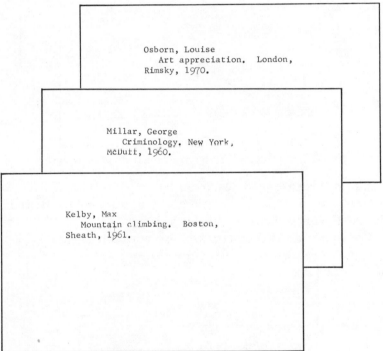

Fig. 6. Three main entries filed alphabetically

These three entries have been correctly filed because they are arranged in rank order. Rank, here, is determined by the alphabetical sequence of the initial letters of the first word in each entry: K<M<O. One criterion of rank order is the alphabetical sequence of letters. As many readers already know, and as we shall discuss in more detail later, rank in filing can be determined by several different criteria. The following two entries are also correctly filed:

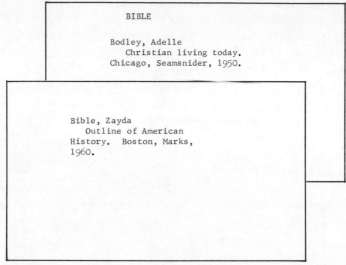

Fig. 7. Two entries filed by meaning instead of alphabet

Rank, in this case, is determined by the context of the word Bible. Bible, a person's last name, is outranked by BIBLE, the same word used as a subject heading.

The following two entries are also correctly filed:

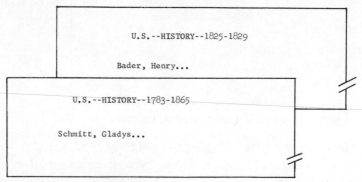

Fig. 8. Two entries filed numerically

As we can see, rank here is determined neither by alphabetical order nor by context, but by still another criterion: the numerical order of a range of dates. These few examples show that there are a number of ways by which rank difference among entries can be determined.

We must stress the importance of "difference" in this context, for each entry must differ in some way from every other entry in the file. Filing ultimately reduces to a decision of rank difference between two compared entries. Thus, it would be a logical impossibility to file two completely identical entries. And if we can agree that filing is a question of rank difference between entries, then we should have no further problem in developing the basic principle of filing library catalog cards. This principle can be captured in one sentence:

Filing a catalog entry is the process of inserting the entry to be filed (the source entry) into a catalog (a target file) in such a manner that the source entry follows a target entry of lower rank but precedes a target entry of higher rank.

We could use some shorthand notation and describe this situation in the following formula:

$$TE_a < SE < TE_p.$$

Here the symbol TE_a stands for the target entry immediately anterior to the source entry SE. And TE_p is the target entry immediately posterior. The inequality signs indicate the ranks of the entries.

This principle, of course, is not new. Only the statement of it is new. The statement as it stands describes the basic characteristic of every correctly filed catalog in the world, past, present, and future. There are no exceptions. And that is as it should be because a basic principle that does not apply to all cases is a contradiction in terms: it is obviously not basic enough.

19

2. Blocks

We have seen that all filing operations are performed on entries. The very first step in filing, it goes without saying then, is to select a source entry, a card that needs to be filed. From a stack of unordered cards waiting to be filed we might, for example, pull this source entry:

```
     Bassham, James Alan.
       The path of carbon in photo-
     synthesis.  New York, McRae, 1957.
       800p.
```

Fig. 9. Author main entry

Let us assume we want to file this example into a conventional dictionary card catalog. The catalog tray that would contain the configuration of elements that we have come to call the "word" Bassham might be labelled as in the illustration in figure 10. Within this tray there might be two guide cards as in figure 11.

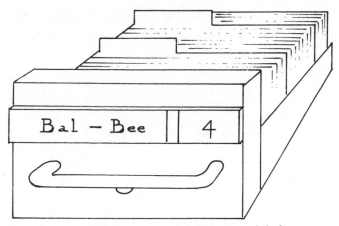

Fig. 10. Typical card catalog tray with range label

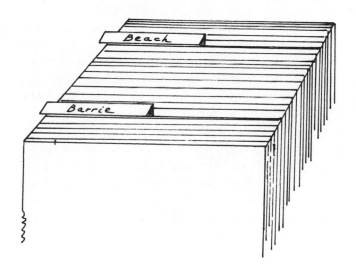

Fig. 11. Typical guide cards in a catalog tray

From this tray we must now select a starting target entry. This might be the following entry, found between BARRIE and BEACH:

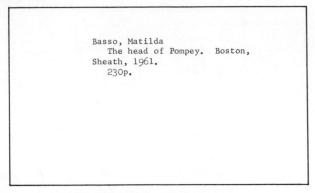

```
Basso, Matilda
    The head of Pompey.   Boston,
Sheath, 1961.
    230p.
```

Fig. 12. Author main entry

We have now a source entry and a target entry to compare. To file, we simply determine whether the source entry belongs in front of or behind the target entry.

But before we can do this we must first select a starting point where to begin the comparison process. This is the next step in filing. And according to common sense and Rule 1.B we begin at the top of the card with the first word. It is easy enough to see that as we attempt to file the card shown in figure 9 we begin with the word "Bassham". It is also obvious that if the target entry with which this card has to be compared is the card of figure 12, we will first look at the word "Basso", not the word "The", for example, or the word "head" or "Boston". In other words, although there are many items on a catalog card, we observe a certain sequence in filing. We pair off source and target items in a very orderly, prescribed manner, beginning at the top of the card, going from left to right.

In the Bassham-Basso example we had no difficulty in deciding to file by the authors' last name. The rank difference between the two entries arose at the very beginning of the comparison process, in the first item. But supposing we had to file cards that were all entered under the same name. For example, let us attempt to file this source entry:

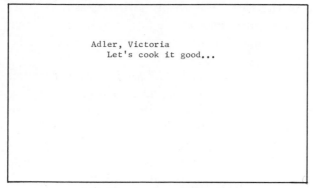

Fig. 13. Author main entry

Let us assume it had to go into this file:

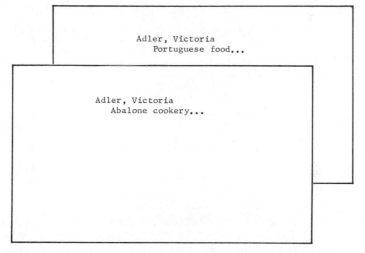

Fig. 14. Two author main entries subarranged by their titles

Obviously, we first compare the authors' names, item by item, and find in this case that there is no difference between source and target entries (Adler=Adler=Adler; and Victoria= Victoria=Victoria). The three names are equivalent and the entries cannot be filed on that basis. In a case like this we apply Rule 26.A.1) and proceed to the next block of information on the card. We continue to file by the title. Here we encounter a difference in the first item and find a place for "Let's cook it good" between "Abalone cookery" and "Portuguese food".

The *concept* of the block as used here is familiar to librarians and many non-librarians. But the *term* "block" in the sense of a unit of bibliographic description as printed or typed on a catalog card is new. It is necessary to introduce this new technical term here because there simply is no other word in common usage that would be generally recognized as designating such a unit of information.

The term "block" presents itself quite naturally because of the characteristic block-like layout of the information on a standard catalog card. Let us look again at an earlier example:

```
Bassham, James Alan
     The path of carbon in photo-
synthesis.  New York, McRae, 1957.
     800p.
```

Fig. 15. Author main entry

This is one of the most prevalent types of cards encountered in a library catalog, the main entry card for a book entered under a personal author. This card contains two distinct units of bibliographic information. One of these units is the author's name. The other unit is sometimes called the title or the body of the entry. These two units are shown here schematically:

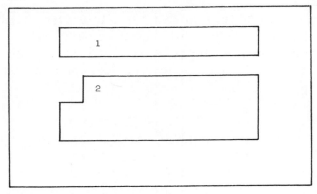

Fig. 16. Schematic representation of a catalog card with the information laid out in two blocks

The block-like layout of the card is easy to recognize. In the drawing we can see that block 1 is the author's name, or "the author", as it is usually called; while block 2 is the unit that includes title and imprint.

There are other blocks to be considered, not shown in this simplified drawing. Figures 17 through 21 are examples of cards laid out in different block configurations.

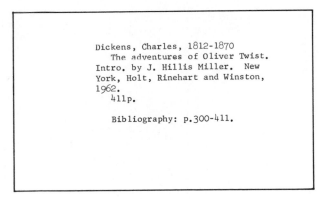

```
Dickens, Charles, 1812-1870
    The adventures of Oliver Twist.
Intro. by J. Hillis Miller.  New
York, Holt, Rinehart and Winston,
1962.
    411p.

Bibliography: p.300-411.
```

Fig. 17. Author main entry

The adventures of Oliver Twist

Dickens, Charles, 1812-1870
    The adventures of Oliver Twist.
Intro. by J. Hillis Miller. New
York, Holt, Rinehart and Winston,
1962.
    411p.

    Bibliography: p.300-411.

Fig. 18. Title added entry

Doe, Joe
    The pony, p.33-45 of

Riner, Jack, ed.
    Twentieth century stories. New
York, Haldeman, 1970.
    311p.

Fig. 19. Author-Title analytic

ELECTRICITY
Roe, Jack
    The electron story, p.220-250 of
Dunes, Damien, ed.
    History of physics. New York,
Willibald, 1965.
    810p.

Fig. 20. Subject-Author-Title analytic

Klotzmeister, Johannes von, 1941-
    [Symphony in G major, Op. 39]
    Kaizer symphony for organ and
trumpets. Victrola 3394.
    Phonodisc. 33 1/3 Stereo

Fig. 21. Author main entry with a uniform title block

Apart from minor deviations, particularly in the question of indentions and spacing, the card layouts shown in figures 17 through 21 are more or less standard in American libraries today. But although the layout is standard, no standard terminology has evolved so far. For example, the second block from the top in figure 22 is sometimes called "the author" or "author's name", sometimes "the main entry", "the heading", or "the catalog entry". Many of these designations are accurate in certain specific situations, but none of them is of general applicability.

```
DICKENS, CHARLES, 1812-1870

Pope-Hennessy, Dame Una (Birch) 1876-1949
    Charles Dickens, by Una Pope-Hennessy.
New York, Howell, 1946.
    488p.

Bibliographical footnotes.
```

Fig. 22. Subject added entry

Mrs. Pope-Hennessy is certainly an author. It is quite correct, therefore, to say that the second block contains an author's name. But Dickens is also an author, and the first block, by that token, also contains an author's name. As a

```
Pope-Hennessy, Dame Una (Birch) 1876-1949
    Charles Dickens, by Una Pope-Hennessy.
New York, Howell, 1946.
    488p.

Bibliographical footnotes.
```

Fig. 23. Author main entry

matter of fact, the third block, too, begins with an author's name. To call the second block on such a card the "author", therefore, would be ambiguous. To call it "the main entry" is also incorrect because that would be the name given to the entire card shown in figure 23. And to call the second block "the heading" is certainly no less confusing since the added entry block is also a heading. What is needed is a unique, logical name for each of the possible blocks found on the standard catalog card.

Let us analyse the phenomenon of the "block" in some detail. Blocks have three major attributes: position, content, and function. *Block position*, as the term indicates, relates to the location of the block on the card. There are five positions:

Added entry blocks
Main entry block
Subsidiary descriptive blocks
Tracings block
Call number block

Diagrammatically, a catalog card can be shown as in figure 24:

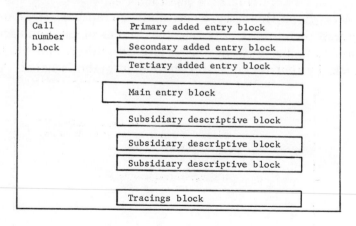

Fig. 24. Schematic of a standard library catalog card,
showing block positions

28

All catalog cards have one main entry block. There are no exceptions. Added entry blocks, one or more, but practically never more than three, are obviously found only on added entry cards. Subsidiary descriptive blocks, one or more, are found on most cards (title blocks, collation block, notes blocks—seldom more than three, but there is no fixed limit). The tracings block and the call number block can be ignored in this discussion since they play no role in filing.

Block content can be divided into four basic kinds: name, name plus title, title, and topic. Here are some examples that show various block contents:

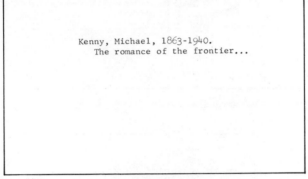

Kenny, Michael, 1863-1940.
    The romance of the frontier...

Fig. 25. Main entry. Main entry block contains a personal name.

Catholic Inter-American Cooperation
        Program.
    Integration of man and society in
Latin America...

Fig. 26. Main entry. Main entry block contains a corporate name.

```
California. Laws, statutes, etc.
    Corporations code annotated of
    the State of California... San
    Francisco, Bancroft-Whitney Co.,
    1962.
        82p.   (Deering's California codes)
```

Fig. 28. Main entry with a main entry block that contains a name plus a title

```
Political intelligence for America's
    future.  Special editor for this
    volume: B. Gross.  Philadelphia,
    1970.
        200p.   (American Eagle Society,
    Publication No. 433)
```

Fig. 30. Main entry with a main entry block that contains a title

```
Newell, Richard Charles, jt. auth.

Newell, Gordon
    Marine plankton, by G. Newell and
    R.C. Newell.  London, Hutchinson, 1963.
        206p.
```

Fig. 27. Added entry with an added entry block that contains a name

```
Beowulf.
    Beowulf.  A new prose translation,
    by Ralph Fuller.  New York, Norton,
    1966.
        58p.
```

Fig. 29. Main entry with a main entry block that contains a title

```
            COTTON GROWING -- ARKANSAS

        Kester, Howard
            Revolt among the sharecroppers.
        New York, Arno, 1969.
            98p.
```

Fig. 31. Added entry with an added entry block
that contains a topical subject heading

Block functions can be divided into three branches: author
blocks, title blocks, and subject blocks. Here are some
examples of different block functions:

```
            Newell, Richard, jt.auth.

        Newell, Gordon
            Marine plankton.   London,
        Hutchinson, 1963.
            206p.
```

Fig. 32. Added entry with an added entry block
functioning as author block

```
            COTTON, JOHN, 1584-1652

        Emerson, Everett
            John Cotton.   New York, Twayne,
        1965.
            176p.
```

Fig. 33. Added entry with an added entry block
functioning as subject block

```
          Aristotle

Taylor, Alfred Edward, 1869-1945.
    Aristotle. Rev. ed.  New York,
Dover, 1956.
    118p.
```

Fig. 34. Added entry with one added entry block
functioning as title block

In addition to these three distinctions, blocks may play
one of two *roles* in a given filing situation: they may be
serving as first filing block or as subsequent filing block.
Logic and common sense dictate that we begin filing on the
first block from the top of a card, the first filing block. Two
blocks only can serve as first filing blocks, the main entry
block and the primary added entry block.

In a main entry card the main entry block is by definition
the first filing block. Here are two examples:

```
          Cotton, Frank
              Advanced inorganic chemistry.
          New York, Interscience, 1962.
              698p.
```

Fig. 35. Main entry. Main entry block contains a
name functioning as author.

```
Crime in urban society, ed. by
    Barbara McLennan.  New York,
    Dunellen, 1970.
    400p.
```

Fig. 36. Main entry. Main entry block contains a
title and functions as title.

In an added entry card the first filing block is always the
primary added entry block. Here are two examples:

```
California.  University, Davis

Food for man in the future; a sym-
    posium.  Berkeley, University
    of California, 1964.
    125p.
```

Fig. 37. Added entry with primary added entry block
serving as first filing block

```
Shaw, George Bernard, 1856-1950.
    Pygmalion.

Downs, Albert
    The six funniest plays of the
British theater... New York,
Dodds, 1954.
```

Fig. 38. Added entry with two added entry blocks.
Primary added entry block serves as first
filing block.

All other blocks, as far as they come into play at all, serve as subsequent filing blocks. They enter into the decision only when the entries compared are equal in respect to the first filing block. Here is a pair of main entry cards subarranged by a subsequent filing block:

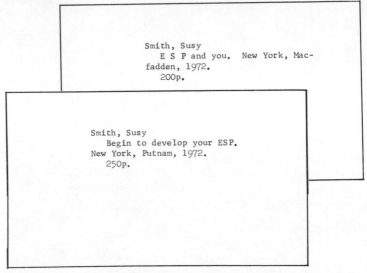

Fig. 39. Two author main entries subarranged by their titles.

By virtue of their key role as first filing blocks, the main entry block and the primary added entry block deserve the special attention of filers. Table 1 shows the possible combinations of content and function in main entry and primary added entry blocks.

Block Position	Block Content											
	Name			Name plus Title			Title			Topic		
	Block Function			Block Function			Block Function			Block Function		
	Author Block	Title Block	Subject Block	Author Block	Title Block	Subject Block	Author Block	Title Block	Subject Block	Author Block	Title Block	Subject Block
Main entry Block	YES	NO	NO	YES	NO	NO	NO	YES	NO	NO	NO	NO
Added entry Block	YES	NO	YES	YES	NO	YES	NO	YES	YES	NO	NO	YES

Table 1. Possible combinations of block content and block function in many entry and added entry blocks

According to the table, it is possible for a main entry block to contain three of the four kinds of content, all except a topic. Obviously, when a main entry block contains a name, that name serves as author information, bibliographically speaking. (This includes editors, translators, compilers, and such.) And when the main entry block contains a title, it serves as title block. The situation is not quite so simple in the case of the primary added entry block. For when a primary added entry block contains a name, that name may convey either authorship or subject information. Likewise, when a primary added entry block contains a title, it may serve either as title block, or as subject block. Here are some cards that exemplify each of these situations:

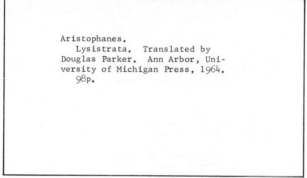

Fig. 40. Main entry. Main entry block contains a name and serves as author block.

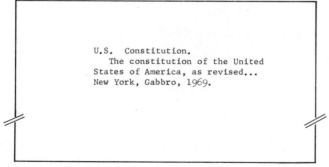

Fig. 41. Main entry. Main entry block contains a name plus a title and serves as author block.

```
Koran.
   The Koran.  Translated  from the
Arabic by J.M. Rodwell... New York,
Dutton [1909]
   506p.
```

Fig. 42. Main entry. Main entry block contains a title and serves as title block.

```
International encyclopedia of chemical
   science.  Princeton, N.J., Van
Nostrand [1964]
   1331p.
```

Fig. 43. Main entry. Main entry block contains a title and serves as title block.

```
Adams, Gary B., ed.

Juvenile justice management.  Edited
by Gary B. Adams... Springfield,
Ill., Thomas, 1973.
   642p.
```

Fig. 44. Added entry. Primary added entry block contains a name and serves as author block.

```
FULLER, HENRY BLAKE, 1857-1929

Bowron, Bernard R.
   Henry B. Fuller of Chicago; the
ordeal of a genteel realist in un-
genteel America.  Westport, Conn.,
Greenwood Press, 1974.
```

Fig. 45. Added entry. Primary added entry block contains a name and serves as subject block.

Franklin, Benjamin, 1706-1790. Poor
    Richard.

Barbour, Frances M.
    A concordance to the sayings in
Franklin's Poor Richard... Gale
Research Co., 1974.

Fig. 46. Added entry. Primary added entry block contains a name plus a title and serves as author block.

Who needs Shakespeare?

Finkelstein, Sidney W., 1909-
    Who needs Shakespeare?...
New York, Interbook [1973]

Fig. 48. Added entry. Primary added entry block contains a title and serves as title block.

DICKENS, CHARLES, 1812-1870. THE POST-
    HUMOUS PAPERS OF THE PICKWICK CLUB

Fitzgerald, Percy H., 1834-1925.
    Pickwickian manners and customs...
New York, Haskell House, 1974.

Fig. 47. Added entry. Primary added entry block contains a name plus a title and serves as subject block.

NIHONGI

Ashton, David G.
    The wisdom of old Japan...
Tuttle [1953]

Fig. 49. Added entry. Primary added entry block contains a title and serves as subject block.

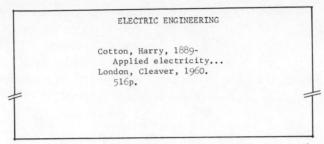

Fig. 50. Added entry. Primary added entry block contains a
topic and serves as subject block.

As the foregoing examples have shown, library catalog
cards come in a bewildering variety of kinds. Unless we
analyse their structure it may seem a mystery why an author
is always a name, but names are not always authors, yet some
authors, while names, are subjects, and so forth. Compli-
cated as all this sounds, it can be reduced to a very simple
general pattern. Since there are two kinds of main entry
blocks, those functioning as author block and those functioning as title block; and since each functional type of main
entry block can appear on four kinds of cards, namely main
entry cards, added entry cards with a single added entry
block, added entry cards with two, and with three added
entry blocks, we arrive at a total of eight possible different
card patterns. These are summarized in table 2.

Main entry block function	Card type			
	Main entry card	Added entry card		
		Number of added entry blocks		
		One	Two	Three
	a	b	c	d
Author block 1	1a	1b	1c	1d
Title block 2	2a	2b	2c	2d

Table 2. Eight possible catalog card layout patterns

38

An understanding of these eight block patterns makes it relatively simple to apply the twenty or so different rules for block selection that are dispersed throughout the *ALA Rules*. To demonstrate, let us examine Rule 26.A.1). This rule directs the filer to subarrange by title. We applied this rule in the "Adler, Victoria" example, repeated here:

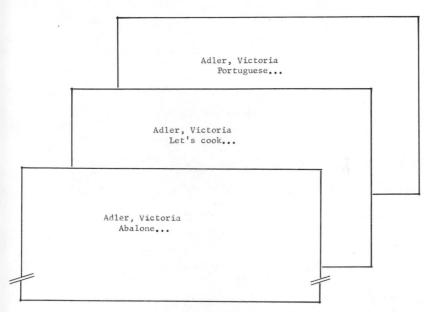

Fig. 51. Three author main entries subarranged by their titles

The example in figure 51 shows three cards of Pattern 1a. The main entry blocks are equivalent. Adhering to the Basic Principle, we subarrange by the next block. Since in cards of this pattern the next block is always a title block, the direction to subarrange by title leads to the same result.

But subarrangement can be more complex, especially in filing situations involving mixed patterns. Supposing we wanted to file the entry shown in figure 52 into the target file shown in figure 53.

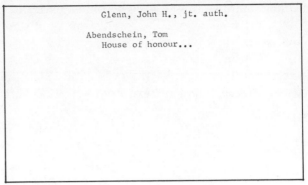

Fig. 52. Author added entry

Fig. 53. Two author main entries subarranged by their titles

If we simply followed the Basic Principle we would file item by item and put the source entry in third place. The resulting order is show in figure 54.

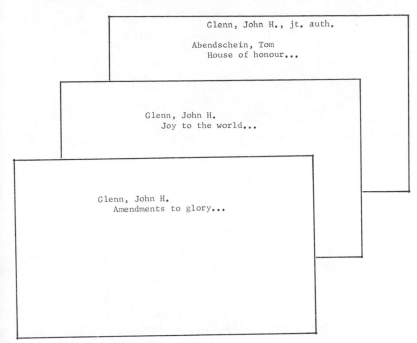

Fig. 54. Three author entries filed according to the
Basic Principle of the *ALA Rules*

However, this is not really what happens. For reasons
discussed later in Chapter 4, we ignore the designation "jt.
auth." in filing and treat the first source block as if it read
"Glenn, John H.". This stratagem equalizes the primary
filing blocks of the three entries under consideration. We are
now forced to look for the next filing block in order to come
to a rank order decision. Again, if we followed Rule 1.B and
simply filed word by word as described, we should reason
that the next word in the source entry (Abendschein) is
clearly outranked by the first word of the first target entry
(Amendments). We should subarrange the entries in this
order: Abendschein→Amendments→Joy. Here is a picture
of the resulting order:

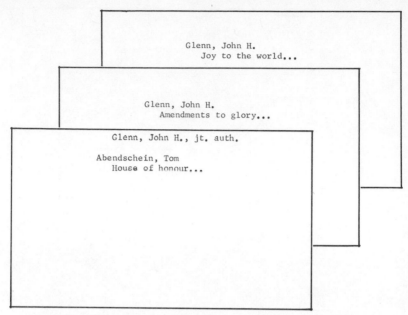

```
                    Glenn, John H.
                       Joy to the world...



               Glenn, John H.
                  Amendments to glory...

        Glenn, John H., jt. auth.

     Abendschein, Tom
       House of honour...
```

Fig. 55. Three author entries filed according to ALA Rule 1.B.

This, however, is not what we do, either. As we reach the end of the added entry block "Glenn, John H." in the source entry without having been able to make a filing decision on the first block we apply a different rule, Rule 26.B.2. We do this because the heading "Glenn, John H., jt. auth." is not an author heading in the sense of Rule 26.A. Instead, it is an added entry in the sense of Rule 26.B.2. This rule directs us to "disregard an author main entry". Undoubtedly, what the compilers of the Rules really meant to say was that we are to disregard the main entry block in cards of Pattern 1.b. If we do this, we find that we subarrange by the title, after all, and could just as well have used Rule 26.A.1). We encounter a rank difference in the first item of the title and place "House" before "Joy" and after "Amendments". Here is a picture of the three cards in correct order:

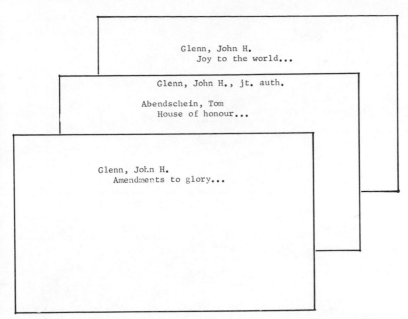

Fig. 56. Three author entries filed according to ALA Rule 26.B.2.

Other situations occur. We encounter entries such as the one depicted in figure 57. If this card were to be compared with the target entry shown in figure 58,

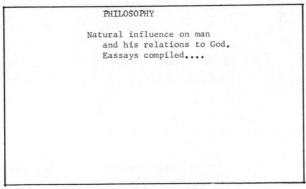

Fig. 57. Subject added entry

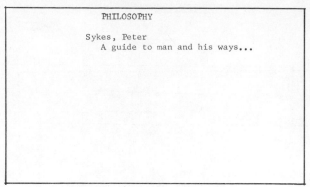

Fig. 58. Subject added entry

we should arrange these two cards according to Rule 32.B in the following order:

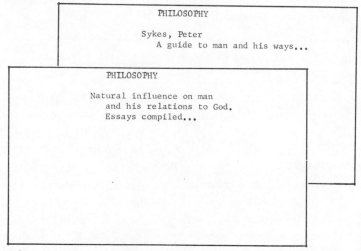

Fig. 59. Two subject added entries filed according to ALA Rule 32.B.

In other words, unlike author added entries, subject added entries are subarranged not by title but by their main entry blocks.

Situations occur where more than the first filing blocks are identical. We might have two entries like those shown in figure 60.

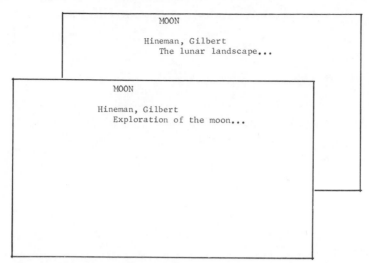

```
                    MOON

          Hineman, Gilbert
            The lunar landscape...

        MOON

   Hineman, Gilbert
     Exploration of the moon...
```

Fig. 60. Two subject added entries subarranged by their titles

According to Rule 32.B we subarrange cards like these (same author) by title.

The last few examples shown above are all related. They deal with the choice of the next filing block if two compared blocks are found to have the same rank. This operation is usually referred to as "subarrangement". The *ALA Rules* treats subarrangement by blocks in at least half a dozen places. Interestingly enough, the term "subarrangement" has escaped the indexers of that book. Nor is the term explained in the Glossary. It is therefore difficult to locate the pertinent rules from case to case. But if we keep in mind that catalog cards come in a limited number of block patterns we can, by a few simple charts, easily explain the process of block selection. Table 3 represents a general guide for the selection of the first filing block.

Here are a few more examples to demonstrate the application of the simple rule presented in the form of table 3. The card in figure 61 is of Pattern 1a. The first filing block, obviously, is the main entry block, "Cotton, Harry".

If the card pattern is...	1a or 2a	1b through 1d, or 2b through 2d
then the first filing block is...	the main entry block	the primary added entry block

Table 3. Criteria for the selection of the first filing block on a catalog card

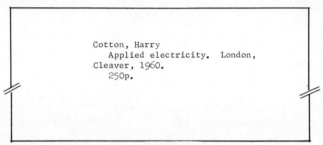

Fig. 61. Author main entry

The card in figure 62 is of Pattern 2b. The first filing block is the added entry block, "McLennan, Barbara, ed."

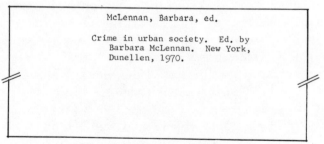

Fig. 62. Author added entry

It is easy enough to determine which shall be the first filing block on a card. Table 4 shows the criteria for the selection of the second filing block in case the first filing blocks on two compared cards are of equal rank.

If the card pattern is...	1a or 2a	1b or 2b		1c,1d,2c, or 2d
and if the primary added entry block functions...	any function	as author block	not as author block	any function
and if the primary added entry block contains...	any contents	a name	a name plus a title	any contents
then the second filing block is...	the next subsidiary descriptive block	the title block	the next block on the card	

Table 4. Criteria for the selection of the second filing block
on a catalog card

Following are two cards with equal main entry blocks. They are of Pattern 1a. These cards, shown in figure 63, are subarranged by the next subsidiary descriptive block:

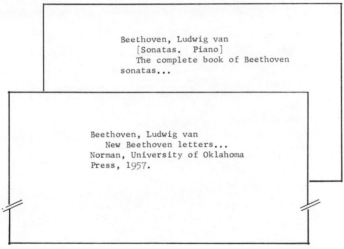

Fig. 63. Two author main entries subarranged by the next
subsidiary descriptive block

Let us consider next two author added entry cards of Patterns 1b and 2b, respectively, with equal primary added entry blocks. In both cards the primary added entry block functions as author block and contains a name. Such cards, true to the criteria set forth in table 4, are subarranged by the title block as shown in figure 64:

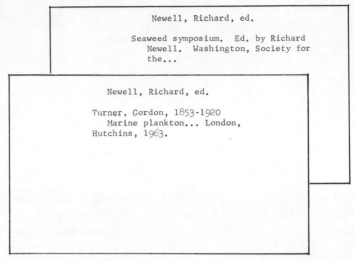

Fig. 64. Two author added entries subarranged by their titles

As a last example, consider two subject added entry cards of Patterns 1b and 2b, respectively. This time the

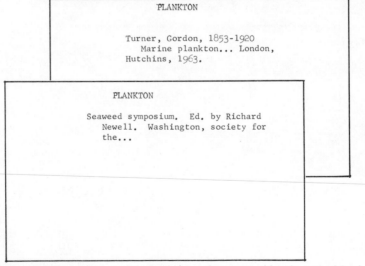

Fig. 65. Two subject added entries subarranged by the next block

primary added entry blocks contain the same topical subject heading. They are subarranged by the next block found on the card, as shown in figure 65:

We notice that subarrangement is always by the next block that is present on the card, with one exception: cards of Pattern 1b. When such an added entry card with a single added entry block has a name in that block, and that block functions as author block, the second filing block is not the next block on the card, but the next block that functions as title block.

A very peculiar further complication arises with cards of this structure when it becomes necessary to select a third filing block. This situation is covered by that masterpiece of an English sentence, Rule 26.B.4: "If under an author heading the title is the same in a main entry for a work by that author and in an added entry under that author's name for a work by another author, or there is more than one added entry with the same title by different authors, arrange the entries for that title under the name as main entry first, followed by the added entries arranged first by the title, then alphabetically by their main entries, then, under the same main entry, chronologically by date."

I offer the following translation: if two author added entries of Pattern 1b are alike in terms of their first and second filing blocks, subarrange by the main entry block.

3. Sections

We have seen that blocks may contain many different kinds of things and serve many functions: there are subject blocks, author blocks, and title blocks; and each of these types of blocks can be of simple or complex structure. The simplest structure is the one-word block. A typical example is the subject block containing a single one-word subject heading:

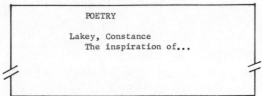

```
        POETRY

    Lakey, Constance
    The inspiration of...
```

Fig. 66. One-word subject heading

Quite often subject headings consist of several words, as, for example, RUSSIAN POETRY. Occasionally such headings are inverted as in SHORT STORIES, RUSSIAN. In filing such entries we follow Rule 1.B and begin with the first word, go to the next word, and so on, paying no attention to punctuation marks. This, undoubtedly, is what the compilers of the *ALA Rules* meant by "straightforward" filing.

But consider another subject heading:

EDUCATION—ALBANIA

Here, too, we have two words separated by a punctuation

mark. Yet these two words are considered as separate sections for filing purposes. This distinction becomes important when we face a mixture of alphabetical and chronological subdivisions. Supposing we wished to file these two entries:

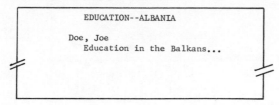

EDUCATION--ALBANIA

Doe, Joe
    Education in the Balkans...

Fig. 67. Geographically subdivided subject heading

and

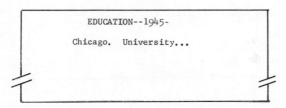

EDUCATION--1945-

Chicago. University...

Fig. 68. Chronologically subdivided subject heading

If we paid no attention to punctuation marks and filed such entries alphabetically according to Rule 1.A, and word by word according to Rule 1.B, we should arrange them in the following order:

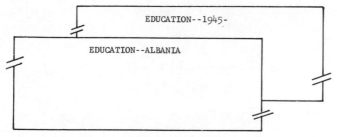

EDUCATION--1945-

EDUCATION--ALBANIA

Fig. 69. Two subject entries filed by Rule 1.

51

Instead, we apply Rule 32.C and file the chronological section before the alphabetical one:

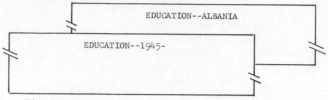

Fig. 70. Two subject entries filed by Rule 32.C.

This we would be unable to do if we had not sectioned the block. The point becomes very clear when we consider the following two entries:

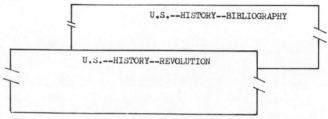

Fig. 71. Two subject entries, chronological before form subdivision

Unless we proceed section by section, and distinguish between alphabetical and chronological sections, there is nothing in these two blocks to signal the correct order.

Yet the sectioning of blocks is not altogether the straightforward matter it appears to be. It would be an oversimplification to say, for example, that a block containing two words separated from each other by commas always constitutes one filing section as in SHORT STORIES, RUSSIAN. This is decidedly not so. Consider these two entries:

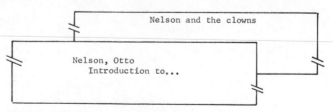

Fig. 72. Two entries filed by Rule 19.A.

Clearly, if Rule 1.B applied and we assumed "Nelson, Otto" to be all one filing section analogous with "SHORT STORIES, RUSSIAN", we should reverse the order, filing "and" before "Otto". However, here we apply Rule 19.A and treat "Nelson," in the main entry block as one filing section, "Otto" as another. We actually file the section "Nelson" before the section "Nelson and the clowns".

But sectioning of author blocks also varies with the kind of punctuation marks used. The block "Nelson, Otto", for example, is sectioned into two filing blocks because we have here two words separated by a punctuation mark. But the block "Nelson-Otto, Zacharias" is not sectioned into three filing blocks, although we do have three words separated by punctuation marks! Instead, "Nelson-Otto" is considered one single filing section. Combining the last three examples we should file as follows:

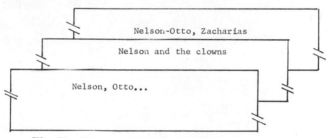

Fig. 73. Three entries filed by Rule 21.A.

We also find catalog entries such as the two that follow:

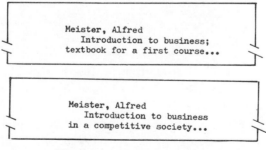

Fig. 74. Two main entries

If we simply filed alphabetically word by word and block by block, we should arrange these two cards in the following order:

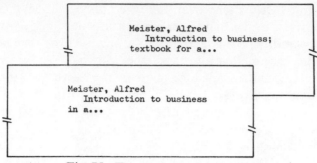

Fig. 75. Two main entries filed by Rule 1.

The rank difference arises in the first subsidiary block, we might say, at the fourth word, "in" vs. "textbook". But this is not what we do. Instead, we divide the block contents into sections. We treat the title proper as one section, and the subtitles as a different filing section. We then file section by section. We apply Rule 26.B.5 and subarrange by the title proper, considering "textbook . . ." as a subtitle. If we do this, we arrive at the correct order:

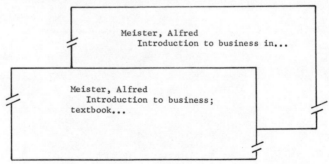

Fig. 76. Two main entries filed by Rule 26.B.5.

Although the *ALA Rules* presupposes the existence of the filing section, no specific mention is made of this concept anywhere, excepting a few passages that call for differential filing according to "groups". We shall therefore make an attempt here to define the phenomenon. First the concept of the typographic section.

A typographic section consists of any non-punctuation symbol (any letter, numeral, or sign such as $, %, or &), or sequence of such symbols, with or without spaces between them, bordered on both sides or on the right by a punctuation mark. The following are examples of typographic sections:

> Cotton.
> Emerson,   (as in "Emerson, Henry")
> Cotton Mather,   (as in "Cotton Mather, keeper
>   of the Puritan conscience")
> The cotton kingdom; (as in "The cotton kingdom;
>   a chronicle of the old South")
> Nelson-   (as in "Nelson-Otto, Henry")
> -Otto,   (as in "Nelson-Otto, Henry")

A special case of typographic section is the simple one-word block, for example POETRY (a word bordered by spaces on both sides).

The typographic section is a visual phenomenon, a mechanical concept. A machine could be made to skim along a sequence of symbols and instructed to mark off a section every time it meets a punctuation mark. Thus, in the list presented above, "Emerson," is a typographic section, a sequence of symbols (E m e r s o n) bordered on the right by a punctuation mark (,). So is "Nelson-", a typographic section because it consists of a sequence of symbols (N e l s o n) bordered on the right by a punctuation mark (-).

A filing section, in contrast to a typographic section, is not nearly as easily defined. Filing sections differ in concept from typographic sections. The filing section is an abstract mental construct. Among the examples given above, "Emerson," and "Nelson-" were identified as typographic sections. But while "Emerson," also happens to be a filing section, "Nelson-" is not. Nor is "Cotton Mather,". Fortunately, human filers are equipped to recognize subtle criteria for section delimitation and are not restricted to what appears printed on the catalog card. A skilled filer sees at a glance whether the typographic sections in a block correspond to filing sections (as in "Nelson,") or not (as in "Cotton Mather,").

As a general guideline, we can suggest that blocks are segregated into filing sections in three situations: (1) when they contain a natural title; (2) when they contain a surname that labels a person or a corporate entity; and (3) when they contain subdivided subject headings.

The term "natural title" requires a word of explanation. A book may, on the title page, show the title *The Tragicall Historie of Hamlet, Prince of Denmarke.* Yet in the catalog this book is entered under the shortened title *Hamlet.* The short title *Hamlet* is known as the uniform title, a concept well established in cataloging. To distinguish this uniform title from the title as it appears "naturally" on the title page I have introduced the term "natural title".

The sectioning of blocks that begin with a natural title, then, can be described as follows:

1. When there is only one main title without subtitles, that title is a filing section.

   Examples:
   > The instruments of music (one section)
   > Intelligence, its evolution and forms (one section)

2. When there is a main title and one or more subtitles, these partial titles are filing sections.

   Examples:

   > Success story; the life of S.S. McClure (two sections)
   > An introduction to personal adjustment; a new approach to guidance and counseling (two sections)

The pertinent passage in the *ALA Rules* is Rule 26.B.5.

The sectioning of blocks that begin with a surname can also be described systematically. But first I must point out that names are of several different types. Names are personal or non-personal. In other words, people or persons have names, but so have things, countries, or companies. While people's names are by definition personal names, the names of things, countries, and other corporate entities can be both, personal and non-personal. Personal names, furthermore, whether they label a person or a corporate entity, can be surnames, given names, or fictitious names; and they can be simple or compound. Also, they may appear in combinations. And corporate-labelling fictitious names, in addition to being compound, may also be single or subdivided. Table 5 attempts to present this amazing array of names in an organized fashion.

	Labelling Persons	Labelling Corporate Entities
Surnames		
Simple	Smith (as in "Smith, Hans Joachim")	Smith (as in "Smith and Son")
Compound	Smith Werner (as in "Smith Werner, Hans")	Smith Werner (as in "Smith Werner Company")
Given Names		
Simple	Aristophanes	
Compound	Hans Joachim	
Fictitious Names		
Simple	Saki	Templars
Compound		
Single	El Greco	Great Britain
Subdivided		U.S. Congress. Senate

Table 5. Different types of names

Names are often qualified by additional information of several kinds. Such qualifiers may be designations that indicate the rank or professional status of a person, or titles of address. Examples are:

Mr.	Father	Sir
Prof.	Bart.	King of Sweden

Some designations indicate the relationship of a person to a work, such as:

ed. comp. jt. auth.

Given names and surnames occasionally carry ordinals:

George VI   Henry Ford III

Dates occur frequently with personal names. They are of three types:

open ranges: 1901-
closed ranges: 1756-1796
point dates: fl. 1099

After these clarifications we can set down the rules for the sectioning of blocks that contain names:

1. When a block begins with a surname that labels a person, and that block contains authorship or subject information (functions as author or as subject block), the surname is a filing section, the given names are another filing section, and the dates, if any, form a chronological section.

    Examples:
    Harvard, William C. (two filing sections)
    PEEL, SIR ROBERT, BART., 1788-1850 (three filing sections)
    Trevor-Roper, Patrick Dacre, 1916-(three filing sections)
    Giner de los Rios, Gloria, ed. (two filing sections)

2. When a block begins with a surname followed by one or more given names that together label a corporate entity, and that block contains authorship or subject information (functions as author or subject block), the

surname is a filing section, the given names are another filing section.

Example:
Magnin, I (firm) (two sections)

3. In all other cases, the entire name is a filing section.

Examples:
Harvard University. William Hayes
Fogg Art Museum (one filing section)
Trevor-Roper and his critics (one filing section)
Peel, Parliament, and the crown (one filing section)

In the *ALA Rules* the sectioning of name blocks is dealt with in Rule 20.

The rules for the sectioning of subdivided subject headings, finally, can be stated very simply:

1. When a block contains an undivided subject heading, the subject heading forms one filing section.

Examples:
POETRY (one filing section)
MEDICINE, PSYCHOSOMATIC (one filing section)
STRESS (PHYSIOLOGY) (one filing section)

2. In subdivided subject headings, all parts are separate filing sections.

Examples:
ROME—HISTORY (two filing sections)
CHURCH HISTORY—1945- (two filing sections)
FRANCE—HISTORY—REVOLUTION, 1789
(three filing sections)

The pertinent passage in the *ALA Rules* is Rule 32.C.

4. Items

Depending on which rule we are following, Rule 1.B or the Basic Principle, we either file word by word or item by item. In chapter 1, when we filed "Millar" after "Kelby", we had no difficulty in recognizing the words Millar and Kelby as filing items. But we must not conclude that all filing items are simply words. If it were so, we should be able to define an item as "a word"; or perhaps more technically as "any sequence of the twenty-six letters of the English alphabet enclosed by spaces or punctuation marks". But while some items are indeed words such as Jonathan, Panovsky, or cheese, other items are not so easily defined, as anyone knows who has ever attempted to file or find a catalog card beginning with or containing an initial ("A" in A.L.A.), an abbreviation ("Mr." in Mr. Roberts), an acronym (UNESCO), a numeral ("4" in 4 sale), a number ("106" in 106 trombones), a prefix ("Du" in Du Barry), a compound (Camp Fire Girls), a date (1984), a range of dates (1933-1945), a period subdivision (REVOLUTION), a sign ($), or a punctuation mark (?).

In fact, the problem has proved so elusive that even after decades of practice and several editions of published filing rules the library profession is still without a precise definition of what constitutes an item, or for that matter, a word.

The skeptical reader might look in the *A.L.A. Glossary of Library Terms* (1943), or in the *Encyclopedia of Librarian-*

ship by Thomas Landau (3rd revised edition, 1968), or in the glossary of the *ALA Rules*. He will find no mention of either term. One recent reference book, *The Librarian's Glossary*, compiled by Leonard Montague Harrod (3rd edition, 1971), does define the term item, but in a different context: as a synonym for document or book. In the same volume, the term "word" is defined as a spoken or written symbol of an idea, which is not precise enough to help a filer decide if the "A" of A.L.A. or the "Camp" of Camp Fire Girls is a word or not. Another recent book, *Filing Rules: a Three-Way Divided Catalog*, by Grant W. Morse (Linnet, 1971) defines word as an element which can stand alone as an utterance. This is similar to Harrod's definition and leaves the same questions unanswered. A very interesting definition of "word" has been proposed by John C. Rather, Chief of the Technical Processes Research Office in the Library of Congress. In his *Filing Arrangement in the Library of Congress Catalogs* (provisional version, 1971), he defines word as one or more characters set off by spaces and/or marks of significant punctuation. This kind of definition, of course, requires another definition, and so Rather defines a "mark of significant punctuation" as one that separates two filing sections in a block, or in his own terminology, one that indicates the end of an element (p.xii).

In the files of the Library of Congress this may be a perfectly sufficient definition. But in terms of the *ALA Rules* it is not adequate. Under Rather's definition, for example, the surname "De los Rios de Garcia Lorca" would consist of six words, six instances of one or more characters set off by spaces. By the *ALA Rules*, however, the entire name is considered one word (Rule 14.A). Or consider the initials AACE. Under Rather's definition these form one word. Under the *ALA Rules'* terms they are four words (Rule 5.B).

Perhaps the time has come to look for a better definition. We should begin by asking what the elements, the simplest parts, of an item are. The answer may come easier if we rephrase the question: what is the smallest thing one can read on a catalog card? To this question we have a ready answer: the smallest thing one can read on a catalog card is a typographic symbol. If catalog cards contain items, and they must since we are directed by the *ALA Rules* to file item by item, then the elements of all items, be they words or numbers or signs or prefixes or any other class we can think of, must be typographic symbols.

Keeping this concept in mind, we can attempt to formulate a new definition of "item":

> An item is any typographic symbol or sequence of such symbols enclosed by spaces.

This definition, practically identical to the one developed by Rather, mentioned above, can easily be tested. Take a fictitious title like *Abacus arithmetic made easy*. Here the items are clear to see. They are all sequences of typographic symbols enclosed by spaces. There are four items involved, the four words Abacus, arithmetic, made, and easy. We can repeat the same test on any number of titles, names, or headings. The definition of "item" appears to be precise and of general applicability. But the prospective filer is warned that several complications lie ahead.

The first of these is the enigma of the "space". We have said that items consist of elements or typographic symbols, and that they are enclosed between spaces. Now, it is a relatively easy matter to spot a typographic symbol, be it a letter, a numeral, a punctuation mark, or any other character the printer's font may hold. But it is far less easy to tell a space. We might say that a space is a gap between letters. But of course there are always gaps between letters (except for ligatures, such as æ or ffi). No two letters on this page touch. Yet we do not recognize these small gaps between letters as spaces. Instead, we settle on an arbitrary gap size standard before we consider the empty paper between two typographic symbols a space. Just what that gap size standard is has never been formulated. Apparently, though, the world has not found this vagueness much of a hindrance since the invention of printing half a millenium ago. And we saw in the "Abacus" example that it was so easy to apply the standard that we did not even notice that we were doing so. We might acquiesce, but there is more to it.

For in filing we find that there are not only visible spaces, however ill defined, but also invisible ones. These invisible spaces might be characterized as gaps between elements that do not approach the customary gap size standard and yet are treated as if they did. Consider another fictitious title, *Abc of lettering*. If we rely on our (inborn?) gap size standard we should segregate three items in this line: Abc, of, and lettering. However, while the gap between A and b in Abc, when measured with a good ruler, is of exactly the same size as the gap between A and b in Abacus, these two groups of elements enclosed by spaces are not treated identically in filing. Obviously, then, we have to do with two different kinds of spaces.

If we designate the visible spaces enclosing the word Abacus by a little triangle ($\triangle$) we might rewrite the item as follows:

$$\triangle \text{ Abacus } \triangle$$

For communications reasons we might find it convenient to name this kind of space a truespace. For the other space we have to invent a different symbol, perhaps an inverted triangle with a tail ($\triangledown$) and call it, since it designates a space that is not visible but latent, as it were, a latentspace. In our example, the word Abc would then have to be rewritten as follows:

$$\triangle \text{A} \triangledown \text{b} \triangledown \text{c} \triangle$$

For the moment, this solves our problem. We simply refine our definition of an item a little:

An item is any typographic symbol or sequence of such symbols enclosed by truespaces or latentspaces.

For filing purposes it is a matter of considerable importance whether a certain sequence of symbols on a catalog card is read, say, as

$$\triangle \, A \triangledown \, b \triangledown \, c \, \triangle (\text{three items})$$

or as

$$\triangle Abc \triangle (\text{one item})$$

If read as three items, Abc files behind "A and B" but before "A is first". If read as one item, on the other hand, Abc would file a certain distance away, behind "Abbot" and before "Abderian".

But the latentspace is not the cure for all filing ills, either. There is another space problem to be considered. For not only have we visible and invisible spaces, we also must reckon with the fact that even visible spaces are not all of the same kind. Consider these two groups of filing elements enclosed by visible spaces:

Los Angeles

Although the paper between the s of Los and the A of Angeles clearly represents a space and the group of symbols "Los" would by our earlier definition be beyond a doubt an item, we find that in this case we consider the space between s and A nonexistent. Consequently, we treat "Los Angeles" as if it were spelled

Losangeles

We can see the space between Los and Angeles, but it is an illusion. It is not really there. For this reason we might call this illusory space a "pseudospace" and invent another symbol for it (Θ). We now rewrite Los Angeles as

$$\triangle Los \, \Theta \, Angeles \, \triangle$$

By this stratagem we uphold our definition and treat "Los Angeles" as one item. We file it between "losable" and "lost". Without the pseudospace we should have identified the item "Los" as an initial article, dropped it according to the rules, and filed Los Angeles between "Angel cake" and "angelic".

So much for the complications that go with the concept of "space" in filing. The second complication arises from the fact that typographic symbols are divided into two classes. The main class are those symbols we commonly regard as visible elements in filing. They are divided into two groups: letters (A a x) and numerals (4 X). This class of symbols possesses rank ordering qualities. Letter A precedes letter B; number 5 comes after number 4. A small subclass are the signs ($ % &). These do occasionally, but not always, enter into the ordering decision.

The second class of typographic symbols are the punctuation marks. Punctuation marks (. , (and many others) do not enter into the ranking decision except in one rare case to be discussed later. In all other instances punctuation marks are either disregarded or regarded as distinguishing marks between sections. If disregarded, they may be made to vanish without a trace as for example in "Wine, women, and song" or "home-coming". When we disregard the punctuation marks in these examples we are left with "Wine women and song" and "homecoming", respectively. But punctuation marks may also disappear and leave an imaginary space in their stead, as in "epoch-making". When we disregard the hyphen in this example we are left with "epoch making".

Punctuation marks regarded as distinguishing marks between sections are found in headings such as "Artz, Frederick" or "The early years; a history of America". A few punctuation marks occasionally do double duty as signs, as in the by-line of this title: *East and West; the confessions of a princess*, by -?.

One of the punctuation marks, the period, serves grammatically to mark the end of filing sections or blocks (*The new English Bible.*) and also to indicate abbreviation (Mr., Harold F.). On occasion this double usage creates minor ambiguities as in this title block, "*History of the U.N.* New York, Neff, 1974.", where the period after the N serves to indicate abbreviation, and also marks the end of a section. But by and large it is true that punctuation marks serve to segregate elements from each other. With this in mind, we might attempt another refinement of our item definition:

An item is any letter, numeral, or sign, or sequence of such symbols, enclosed by truespaces, latentspaces, and/ or punctuation marks.

By this last definition all of the following seven blocks can be seen to contain four items each:

1. Abacus arithmetic made easy
2. U.S.—HISTORY—REVOLUTION
3. Man, beast, and life
4. The first Mrs. Miller
5. Knut, King of Denmark
6. The Spirit of 1984
7. This * * war

The definition, however, is only a starting point. The myriad exceptions that occur in practice have spawned a clutter of detailed special provisions in the *ALA Rules* which it is extremely difficult to survey. These exceptions are due to three causes. First, truespaces are hard to spot since not all visible spaces are truespaces, as we have seen. This phenomenon of a space that isn't a space can be considered a problem of compounds. Compounds are discussed in the *ALA Rules* under a variety of rule numbers, notably Rules 11, 13, 14, 21, 22, 23, 25. However, item definition can be simplified as follows:

If the item isolated by applying the definition of page

66 forms a compound with one or more of the surrounding items, the entire compound constitutes one filing item.

Secondly, the latentspace, not being visible at all, is even harder to spot. This phenomenon is covered in the *ALA Rules* under Rule 5. The definition of this·kind of item can be simplified as follows:

If the item isolated by applying the definition of page 66 consists of a series of abbreviations printed without visible spaces between them, each abbreviation is a filing item.

The third cause is the lack of precision concerning punctuation marks. Rule 3 covers this subject, but not exhaustively. It presents an enumeration of punctuation marks that ends with "etc.", and this is bound to leave questions unanswered when there is a need to be definite. Here is an attempt to pin down the criteria by which punctuation marks define items:

If the item isolated by applying the definition of page 66 is bordered on at least one side by one of the punctuation marks listed below it is a filing item

period	parenthesis	question mark
comma	bracket	exclamation point
colon	semicolon	quotation mark
dash	virgule (slash)	

If the item is bordered on at least one side by a hyphen, and this item and its immediate neighbor on the hyphen side form a compound, the compound is a filing item. If they don't form a compound, each item is a separate filing item.

If the item contains apostrophes, these are ignored entirely; they are treated as if they had vanished without leaving a space.

Here are a few examples to illustrate how these guidelines work. Consider this block:

De los Rios de Garcia Lorca, Laura, jt. ed.

Beginning at the left, we isolate the sequence of symbols

De

enclosed by truespaces as an item. This item forms a compound with the following five items according to Rule 14.A. Therefore the entire compound is a filing item:

De los Rios de Garcia Lorca (one item)

Now contrast this with a similar block:

Giner de los Rios, Gloria, ed.

Beginning at the left again, we isolate an item:

Giner

Since according to Rule 13.A this item does not form a compound with the following ones, it is a filing item all by itself:

Giner

The reader should notice that the fact that "de los Rios" is a part of both names has nothing to do with item delimitation. The sole criterion in this case is whether or not the items form a compound.

Here is an example to show the treatment of the apostrophe. Consider the source item "I'm" in the block "I'm

OK, you're OK". Let us pretend we had to compare this with the target block

I am Omar's guest

which, we shall further assume, is followed in the file by an entry with this filing block:

Image and experience

The source item "I'm" contains an apostrophe between I and me. This apostrophe vanishes and the item becomes

Im

Now the first item in the first target block is "I". The first item in the second target block is "Image". Therefore, since the mentally transformed first source item now reads "Im", the source entry is filed between the two target entries as shown:

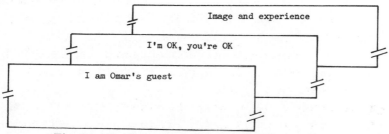

Fig. 77. Three title added entries filed by Rule 7.A.

All too often, when we have succeded in deciding that by all the rules and guidelines at our disposal a given group of symbols constitutes a filing item, as for example the "I" in

William I, Emperor of Swobodia

we find that we still cannot file by this item. We must therefore learn to distinguish items that can be filed from those that can not be filed, another complication of library filing.

Items that can not be filed abound on catalog cards. While they look exactly like regular filing items they are treated as if they were not there. They are pseudo-items. To tell the difference is an intellectual process that requires much study, background knowledge, familiarity with languages, and a certain feeling for context.

The *ALA Rules* cover the subject of pseudo-items under a large variety of rule numbers, notably Rules 1, 4, 5, 8, 11, 13, 14, 15, 20, 25, 26, 33, and 36. This collection of rules suggests what can happen when a system is "improved" by patching. Consider the well-known exception to Basic Rule 1.B. We are instructed to disregard (i.e. regard as pseudo-items) initial articles. This same direction is repeated again in Rule 4.A.1, but several exceptions are added there. In as much as 4.A.1 is already an exception to Rule 1.B, these exceptions are actually exceptions to an exception: regard all words, except initial articles, except certain ones . . .

When we come to Rule 4.A.2 we find that certain initial articles are further excepted from the exception to 4.A.1. The hierarchy now extends to the exception to an exception to an exception to a rule. Just then we are told to except Dutch 's from this last exception. Exactly what level of exception this constitutes has probably never been resolved. The matter seems to lie beyond the realm of reasonable human discourse.

Interestingly enough, while the above-mentioned exception to Rule 1.B refers specifically to initial articles in an entry, we find that articles at the beginning of subject subdivisions and articles following the comma at the end of a heading, although clearly not initial articles in the sense of Rules 1.B and 4.A.1, are nevertheless included among the pseudo-items by a special clause in Rule 4.B.

The rules governing many of the other pseudo-items are not less eccentric. We treat, for example, as pseudo-items all designations following names, but only when they are not needed to distinguish between otherwise identical names

(Rule 20.E.5). The same conditional pseudo-item status belongs to ordinals following given names, as in

CHARLES V, EMPEROR OF GERMANY

(Rule 25.A.2). An intriguing case is the second given name between an ordinal and a designation such as "Adolf" in

GUSTAV II ADOLF, KING OF SWEDEN

which is a pseduo-item (Rule 25.A.4). And although Rule 1.B says expressly that the filer is to "begin with the first word, . . . then go to the next word", we except an author's name at the beginning of a title, provided it functions as an author statement, i.e. is not an integral part of the title (Rule 26.B.6.).

Designations showing relationship of person to work are also pseudo-items (Rule 26.B.3). Some common examples are

ed.	jt. ed.
jt. auth.	comp.
jt. comp.	tr.
illus.	

One of the more esoteric pseudo-items is the name in parentheses that follows the date for a chief of state (Rule 36.E.1). This is by no means the end of the list of pseudo-items. We have not mentioned signs, titles of nobility, and epithets; medium designations (e.g. "phonodisc"), certain subtitles and edition numbers, and titles of office following a name.

It is doubtful if anyone has ever understood or even read all the conditions under which, by the *ALA Rules*, an item is considered a pseduo-item. The network of rules being so dense, and the indexing so thin, the pseudo-item remains a mystery even to many experienced filers. Most libraries, therefore, have cut at least part way through this tangle by superimposing simplified home-made rules. Since there appears to be no general principle that would govern the myriad decisions to regard or not to regard items, in cases of doubt a good many practitioners have reverted to the Basic Rule: they simply file word by word.

5. Ordering Principles

In chapter 1 we determined that filing was essentially a question of rank order among entries. In chapters 2, 3, and 4 we developed steps to select blocks, isolate sections, and identify items. We must now consider how rank order between items is determined.

Rank in filing is a mathematical concept. When we determine the relative positions of items like 1871 and 1933 in two otherwise identical historical subject headings we do so on the basis of their magnitudes. The number 1871 precedes the number 1933 in numerical rank. We say that 1871 is less than 1933, or in symbols,

$$1873<1933$$

In other words, basic order in filing is numerical.

This statement only *appears* to contradict the widely held belief that filing order is basically alphabetical. Granted, the statement that basic order is numerical does not immediately explain why we placed "Millar" after "Kelby", for example. We are tempted to revoke the statement and say that we simply filed those two entries alphabetically. After all, did we not compare the items symbol by symbol, find that "M" outranked "K", and on that basis arrange "Millar" after "Kelby"?

But strictly speaking, there can be no such thing as alphabetical order simply because the symbols that make up the various alphabets of the world have no intrinsic order. There is nothing in the letters A, O, and Z, for example, that would put them in this order. The English alphabet happens to go from A to Z. The Greek alphabet, on the other hand, goes from A to O. The letter Z comes somewhere in the middle. And the Russian alphabet begins *and* ends with A (A and Я), both O and Z being in the middle. It seems that the arrangement of the letters of our alphabets is purely arbitrary.

But of course there is a trick. It is true that we arrange the letters of the English alphabet "in their alphabetical order". If we look carefully, however, we can see that we actually use the arithmetic sequence of the counting numbers from 1 to 26 to put those symbols in order. We simply map our twenty-six letters, one for one, to the sequence of the first 26 counting numbers. After this operation, when the letters A, O, and Z have been equated with the numbers 1, 15, and 26, we can easily put them in order, namely 1, 15, 26. For conversation's sake it is all right to delude ourselves and say that we have filed A, O, and Z in alphabetical order as long as we remember that by this statement we mean that we actually put the mapped letters A, O, and Z into the numerical sequence 1, 15, 26; that we really filed them numerically. In alphabetical filing, F follows E because $6>5$; and "bat" files before "bit" because $a=1$, $i=9$, and $1<9$.

Here is a table to show how we map the twenty-six letters of the English alphabet so that we may file them:

1 A	10 J	19 S
2 B	11 K	20 T
3 C	12 L	21 U
4 D	13 M	22 V
5 E	14 N	23 W
6 F	15 O	24 X
7 G	16 P	25 Y
8 H	17 Q	26 Z
9 I	18 R	

So-called alphabetical filing, then, is a special case of numerical filing, restricted to the range of integers from +1 to +26. The great majority of items are filed by this principle which explains the rise of the popular if unprecise notion that basic order in filing is alphabetical.

A good many items occur in filing, however, that are not filed by mapping symbols to the system of counting numbers from 1 to 26. They are items that express a numerical quantity per se and are ranked by their value. This principle is known as numerical filing. Numerical filing extends over the full range of the rational numbers. There are two methods of numerical filing, though: point filing and range filing. Point filing is the simpler of the two methods. For example, if two headings are alike up to a numerically filed item, the two headings are filed by the numerical values of these items, lesser value first:

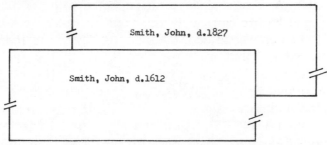

Fig. 78. Two author main entries subarranged chronologically

In range filing we must consider two components, the beginning point of the range ("1882" in 1882-1936) and the endpoint ("1936" in 1882-1936). If two compared ranges have different beginning points, the entries are filed by the numerical values of their beginning points. For example,

Dumas, Alexandre, 1802-1870

files before

Dumas, Alexandre, 1824-1895

75

If two compared ranges have the same beginning point, they are filed by the numerical value of their endpoints, but in reverse order. Thus, the range "1800-1850" files before the range "1800-1840". Incidentally, the range "1800- " files before both of these because the space after the hyphen is mentally translated to ∞ (infinity), which obviously outranks 1850.

Numerically filed entries and alphabetically filed ones are kept separate from each other in library catalogs. Numerical subdivisions precede alphabetical subdivisions in rank. Thus, all the chronological divisions of

U.S.—HISTORY

are filed in a cluster before the alphabetical ones:

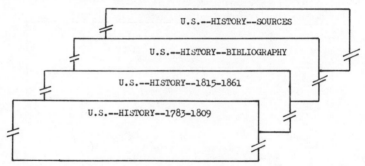

Fig. 79. Four subject entries

In straight numerical filing, items are ranked by their numerical values. In alphabetical filing they are ranked by their numerical values after their elements have been mapped to the system of counting numbers from 1 to 26.

There is a third method of numerical filing. It occurs very seldom and there is only one single mention of it in the *ALA Rules* (Rule 37.B.4). By this method, punctuation marks and spaces are mapped to the counting numbers from 1 to 6 as follows:

1 closing bracket
2 semicolon
3 period
4 parentheses
5 comma
6 space

Under this rule, otherwise identical entries are ranked by the mapped values of their punctuation marks.

If numerical order is the primary ordering principle in library catalogs, it is, alas, not the only principle. There is a secondary ordering principle which is of considerable importance. It ranks entries on the basis of the meaning of a word or the context in which it stands. Because of this I have named the principle "contextual rank order". This principle often overrides numerical order when two compared sections are equivalent in item and symbol content. The principle is best demonstrated by means of an example.

Let us assume we had this source block:

Gray, Thomas

which we might wish to compare to the target block

Gray; the Eton years

Since the first source section is symbolically equivalent to the first target section (Gray=Gray) we would, in the absence of the principle of contextual rank order, proceed to compare the blocks on the basis of the items in the next section. In traditional terminology this would be called "filing straightforward". We would expect to file the source entry after the target entry because "Thomas" outranks "the". But in a case like this the principle of contextual rank order enters into the decision process and the first item pair (Gray, Gray) is actually evaluated by context. Here, the source item Gray is a name functioning as author, while the target item

Gray is a name functioning as title. Hence, the source entry is filed before the target entry, not behind it:

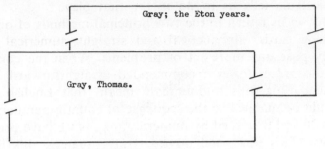

Fig. 80. Two entries filed by Rule 33.A.

In the *ALA Rules*, this situation is covered by Rule 33.A.

Considerations of context dictate other deviations from alphabetical order. Had we been faced with a target file containing this heading:

GRAY, THOMAS   (a subject heading)

the source entry "Gray, Thomas . . ." would still have filed ahead of the target entry even though in terms of symbolic composition the entire source block and the target block are equivalent (Gray, Thomas = GRAY, THOMAS). The principle of contextual rank order places "Gray, Thomas" (the name as author) before "GRAY, THOMAS" (the name as subject). In the *ALA Rules* this falls under Rule 26.A.

Another situation in which order is determined by context is covered by Rule 20.C which directs filers to place a surname followed by a designation after the surname followed by a date. We also arrange an entry for a non-book after an equivalent entry for a book (Rule 37.A). Since the *ALA Rules* makes use of the principle of contextual rank order and at the same time denies its existence, it is hard to collect all the rules that cover the many situations in which rank order is assigned to items on the basis of context. Because of this lack of direction one sees many library catalogs in which the fine points of contextual rank order are simply ignored, and blocks, sections, and items are filed according to what is printed on the card, which, after all, is what the Basic Rule tells us to do in the first place.

But let us return to the two principal methods of ordering catalog cards, alphabetical and straight numerical filing. They pose one more set of problems. When the compilers of the *ALA Rules* recommended straightforward alphabetical filing, this undoubtedly meant that English letters should be mapped to the sequence of countig numbers from 1 to 26 and then filed by numeric rank, as we have proposed above. This was good advice. Unfortunately, this is only possible for items that are composed entirely of mappable alphabetic symbols, i.e. letters of the English alphabet.

Now, while it is true that all items are composed of typographic symbols, they are not all composed entirely of letters of the English alphabet. Consider items such as øre or 1984, for example, or Hank's or Charles V. Among these we encounter several symbols that are not mappable, such as the Danish ø, the numerals, and the apostrophe. Items containing such symbols must be transformed before they can be filed.

One large group of unmappable symbols are the letters pertaining to other alphabets than the English. They are of four kinds. Some are modified versions of the same Latin letters of which the English alphabet is composed, such as German ö or the Danish ø. These modified letters are equated with their unmodified counterparts in the English alphabet, mapped, and interfiled with their counterparts. Thus ö becomes o, which is mapped to 15 (Rule 2.A.1).

Another group are the letters of non-English alphabets such as Greek ω . These are translated into English equivalents, if any, or sounded and spelled in English, and then mapped and filed. Thus ω becomes o, which is mapped to 15 (Rule 1.A). There is a rare subclass of non-English letters that requires special care. The letters in this subclass look like those in the English alphabet but have different equivalents and therefore different numerical ranks. An example is

P, the Greek letter rho. This letter P becomes R, which is mapped to 18. Rules 1.A. and 2.C.5 cover such situations.

Then there are symbols that look like letters of the English alphabet but are in reality non-alphabetical symbols, such as V (Roman 5), which is different from V (letter vee). Rule 9.A.3 treats of such pseudo-letters. Rule 18.B describes still another kind of pseudo-letter which is treated as if it did not exist. The only example shown in the *ALA Rules* is the "h" in Baghdad, which is filed as if spelled Bagdad.

At the opposite end of the spectrum are the "missing" symbols". These are letters that are not printed and therefore cannot be seen; yet the items are treated as if the symbols were there. We mentally insert them. Thus, "McGraw" is filed as if it were spelled "Macgraw"; and "Mr." as if spelled "Mister". In the *ALA Rules*, this phenomenon of the missing symbol is treated by Rules 6.A.1 and 14.B.

The remaining class of unmappable symbols that we must account for in alphabetical filing are the non-alphabetic typographic symbols that include the signs (such as $ and %) and the numeals (such as 5 or V). For alphabetical filing, these non-alphabetic symbols have to be translated. This is done by sounding or speaking what the symbols stand for, spelling out the result in English letters, and mapping and filing those letters in the usual way. By that process of translation "%" is filed as if it were spelled "percent". Rule 8.E covers such translations.

Numerals that are to be filed alphabetically are treated in the same way. They are translated into words; the word is spelled out in terms of the English alphabet; and the result is mapped and filed. We say we file "5" as if spelled "five". Here are two hypothetical headings in proper order according to Rule 9.A:

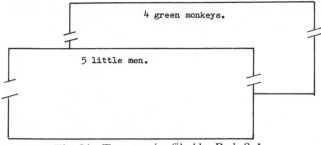

Fig. 81. Two entries filed by Rule 9.A.

Numerical filing, as opposed to alphabetical filing, has its own peculiarities. Strictly speaking, numerical filing can be done only with items that consist entirely of numerical symbols. In the subject heading

NEW ORLEANS. BATTLE OF, 1815

the item "1815" is a pure numerical item. This heading would file before

NEW ORLEANS, BATTLE OF, 1862

the two headings being filed in ascending order by the value of their numerical items.

But not all numerically filed items consist of purely numerical symbols. Some are composed of numerical and alphabetical symbols such as "7th" in "7th Air Force". Such items must be transformed to pure numbers, mentally, before they can be filed numerically. Thus "7th" is filed as if written "7" (Rule 36.E.5). Another example of a mixed numerical item is "50 B.C.". This has to be read as if it were written "-50" (negative fifty). After this mental transformation it files between -55 and +25 (or 55 B.C. and 25 A.D. in conventional terminology). This phenomenon is covered by Rule 32.G.1.

Some numerically filed sections consist entirely of non-numerical items. An example is

CIVIL WAR

in the subject heading

U.S.—HISTORY—CIVIL WAR

The filer must apply a knowledge of history and mentally transform this section into the range

1861-1865

before such a heading can be filed (Rule 32.G.2).

Still another peculiarity of numerical filing arises from the fact that not all numerical items occupy fixed, real positions in an entry; some just seem to be located in their places. For filing purposes they are treated as if they were located elsewhere. We might call this class of items the items that occupy pseudo-positions. For example, the numerically filed item "1935" in "1935 legislative proposals" occupies a pseudo-position. While it is printed before the word "legislative", it is filed as if it were printed after the word "proposals". This strange phenomenon is covered by Rule 36.B.2.a.

The body of rules and exceptions that govern item transformation is large and unwieldy. In addition to the few examples we have just given, the following rules were also created for similar item transformations: 3, 5, 6, 7, 10, 12, 20, 23, and 31. It appears that all of these were formulated ad hoc to clear some particular obstacle as it occurred in the codification process of the filing rules. No systematic plan seems to underly the *ALA Rules* in this area and no generally applicable basic guidelines to item transformation can be given.

6. Flow of Decisions

We have seen that the filing process requires a series of basic decisions concerning filing blocks, sections, items, ordering principles, and transformations. These decisions have to be made in a certain sequence. Incorporating the principles discussed in the preceding five chapters, we present in figure 82 the sections of a step-by-step flow chart designed to visualize the entire operation of filing a card into a dictionary catalog.

All steps or boxes in this flow chart have been numbered by Arabic numerals to facilitate communication. Round connector boxes with capital letters lead to other steps on the same page. Square connector boxes with capital letters lead to remote steps on different pages.

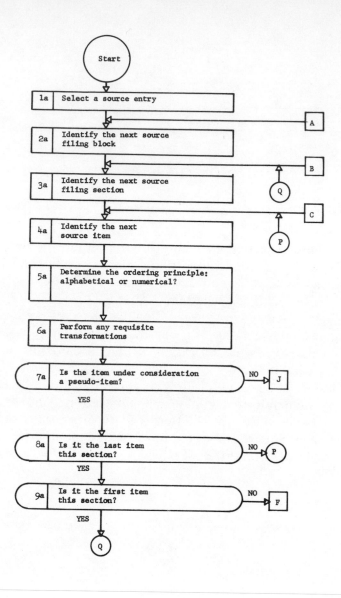

Fig. 82. Flow chart of the filing process

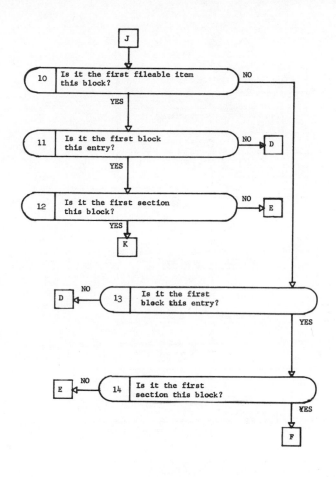

Fig. 82. Flow chart (continued)

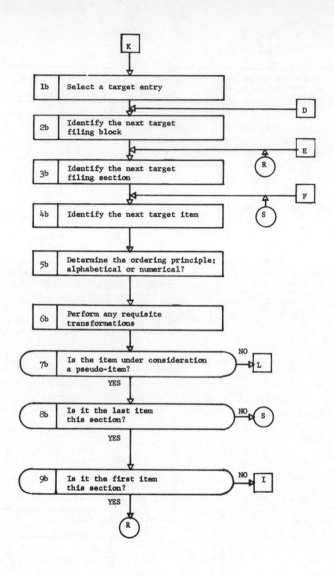

Fig. 82. Flow chart (continued)

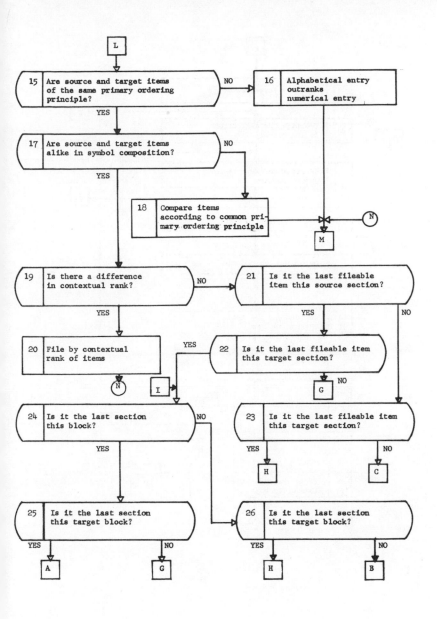

Fig. 82. Flow chart (continued)

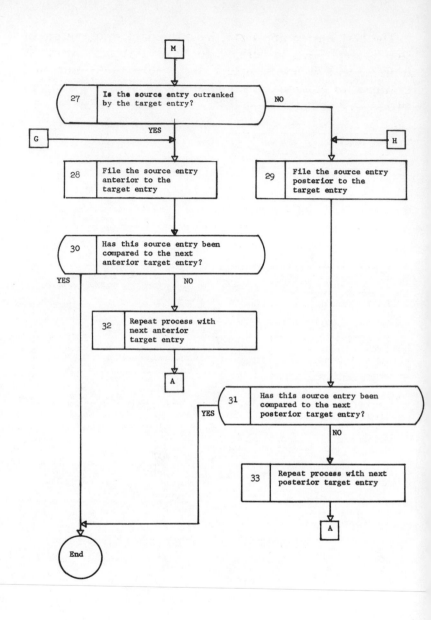

Fig. 82. Flow chart (concluded)

The best way to approach this formidable-looking set of step-by-step charts is perhaps to "walk through" them, as it were, with a few sample filing problems. As our first example we present this miniature target file consisting of two subject added entry cards:

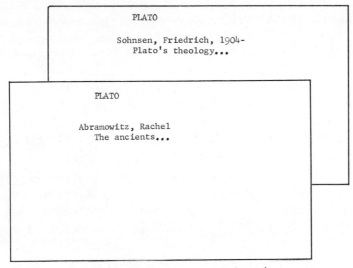

Fig. 83. Two subject added entries

Let us see what happens as we file this source entry (Step 1a):

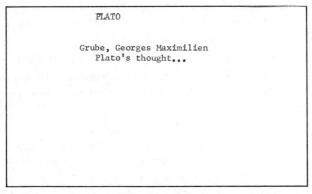

Fig. 84. Subject added entry

As we go to step 2a we ask ourselves: what is the next source block? Obviously, the subject heading, or more technically, the primary added entry block, is the next source block: PLATO. Step 3a is quickly passed since block and section are identical in this case: PLATO. Also Step 4a: section and item are identical. At Step 5a we decide that PLATO is filed alphabetically. At Step 6a we decide that no transformations are needed, PLATO being composed entirely of letters of the English alphabet. At Step 7a we ask if PLATO is a pseudo-item. The answer is no, which brings us to Step 10.

At Step 10 we decide that PLATO is indeed the first item in this block that can be filed and go to Step 11. It is also the first block in this entry, which takes us to Step 12. Here we decide that PLATO is the first section in this block, which takes us to the connector box K.

We have now arrived at Step 1b. At this point we must select a starting target entry. Let us pick the first one, "Abramowitz . . .". At Step 2b we ask ourselves: what is the next target block? Obviously, the primary added entry block, PLATO, is the next target block. Steps 3b through 7b, are in every respect analogous to Steps 3a through 7a, and we need not dwell on the details any longer. This takes us to connector box L.

We have now reached Step 15. Here we begin to compare source and target items. This is in accord with Rule 1, "filing is item by item". The question at Step 15 is: are these two items, PLATO and PLATO, alike in terms of primary ordering principle? The answer is yes, they are both filed alphabetically, as we had determined at Steps 5a and 5b. This takes us to Step 17. The question here is: are these two items alike in terms of symbols? The answer is yes, they are. We go to Step 19.

We must now decide if there is a contextual rank difference between the source item PLATO and the target item PLATO. Both are given names functioning as subject headings. There is no contextual rank difference.

What we have are two blocks that cannot be filed because there is absolutely no difference between them. We go to Step

21 and ask if the source item PLATO is the last one in its section. The answer is yes. At Step 22 we get the same answer for the target item. Steps 24 and 25 confirm that source and target items are the last sections in their blocks, and this takes us to connector box A. We find ourselves back at Step 2a again. Now we need to make use of certain criteria we developed in chapter 2. We see that our source entry is a card of pattern 1.b with the primary added entry block functioning as subject block. According to table 4, the second filing block is the next block on the card, in this case the main entry block.

At Step 3a we must identify the next source section. This takes us back to chapter 3. If we refer to the guidelines given on page 58 we find that "Grube" is the next source section since it is a surname that labels a person, in a block that functions as author block.

In Steps 4a through 6a we decide in quick succession that "Grube" is the next source item, that it is filed alphabetically, and that it needs no transformations. In Step 7a we determine that it is not a pseudo-item. Which takes us to Step 10. We find that "Grube" is the first item in this block that can be filed. In Step 11 we determine that the main entry block of which "Grube" is a section is not the first block in the entry. This takes us to connector box D.

The next decision takes place at Step 2b: what is the next target block? We do not have to go through all this since the determination of the next target block follows the same steps we took to determine the next source block. We determine that "Abramowitz" is the next item and go to connector box L.

We are at Step 15 once more. This time we are asked if "Grube" and "Abramowitz" follow the same ordering principle. They do, and we go to Step 17. Are "Grube" and "Abramowitz" alike in symbol composition? They obviously are not. This decision takes us to Step 18. We are directed to file the two entries by the alphabetical rank of the items "Grube" and "Abramowitz". As we saw in chapter 5, this is done by mapping. We reason as follows: G=7, and A=1, therefore A<G. Hence, the source entry files posterior to the target entry, as we shall see if we follow connector box M to Steps 27 and 29. Here is a picture of the target file at the completion of Step 29:

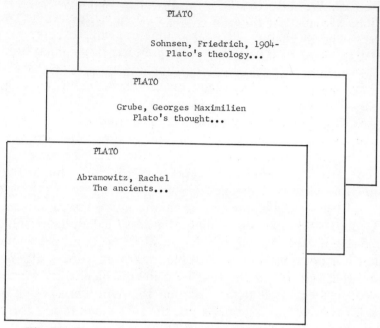

Fig. 85. Three subject added entries subarranged by authors

But let us finish with the flow chart. In Step 31 we ask if we are all done. Since we have placed our source entry into this position:

$$TE_a<SE$$

but have not yet determined the relationship of the source entry to the next entry in the posterior position (here: "Sohnsen . . ."), we go to Step 33 and repeat the entire procedure, beginning with the first source block PLATO at Step 2a (Connector box A). When we reach Step 1b on this round, we select the "Sohnsen" entry as target entry.

I shall not weary the reader by walking through the entire

chart again. Obviously, these two cards are of the same pattern as in the previous pair. We shall arrive at Step 27 and decide that the "Grube" entry is outranked by the "Sohnsen" entry, since G=6, S=19, and therefore G<S. This takes us to Step 29. We have one more decision to make at Step 31. Since we have just finished comparing the "Grube" entry to the "Sohnsen" entry, the answer is yes, and we have arrived at last at the "end" bubble. We have completed the cycle and our little three-card catalog is now correctly filed.

The purpose of the second example is to show what happens at Steps 17 and 18 when the ordering principle is not alphabetical. We have a source entry,

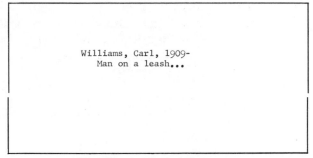

```
Williams, Carl, 1909-
    Man on a leash...
```

Fig. 86. Author main entry

and another hypothetical two-card target file,

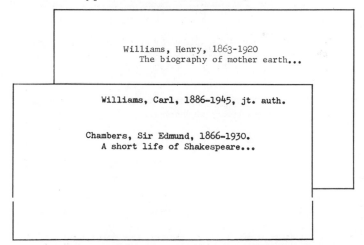

```
Williams, Henry, 1863-1920
    The biography of mother earth...
```

```
Williams, Carl, 1886-1945, jt. auth.


Chambers, Sir Edmund, 1866-1930.
    A short life of Shakespeare...
```

Fig. 87. Two author entries subarranged by given names

93

Obviously—and we do not have to go step-by-step through the whole chart for this—the first block in the source entry (Williams, Carl, 1909-) is identical to the first block in the first target entry (Williams, Carl, 1886-1945, jt. auth.) up to the date. According to the principles of numerical filing explained in chapter 5 we decide at Steps 17 and 18 that the two compared items are not alike and file the entries by the numerical rank of these items,

$$1886 < 1909$$

Following connector box M to Step 29, we place the source entry between the two target entries.

Here is a third example that shows how to deal with pseudo-items. Let us say we had this source entry:

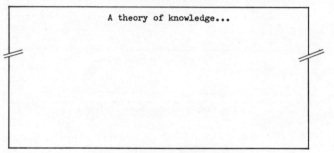

Fig. 88. Title added entry

and a target file containing these two adjacent entries:

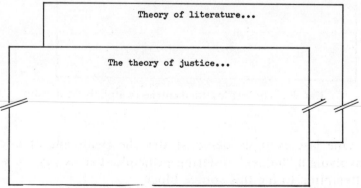

Fig. 89. Two title added entries in alphabetical order

94

As we reach Step 7a on the first time around the flow chart we determine that the "A" of "A theory of knowledge" is a pseudo-item. This decision takes us to Step 8a. The pseudo-item "A" is not the last item in the section. Therefore we follow the arrow to connector box P which takes us up to Step 4a again. We simply pick the next source item, "theory", and continue to file. As we reach Step 7b we encounter another pseudo-item, the article "The" in the first target block. Step 8b sends us via connector box S to Step 4b and we pick the word "theory" as next target item.

From here on the operation is standard. We go through several more loops in the chart until we reach Step 29, filing the "knowledge" entry posterior to the "justice" entry. Here is a picture of the three cards in final order:

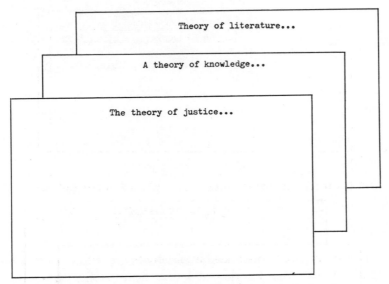

Fig. 90. Three title added entries in alphabetical order

One last example demonstrates the treatment of a case involving a "hidden" ordering principle. Let us say we were attempting to file this source block:

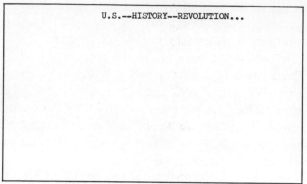

Fig. 91. Subject added entry

into the following target file:

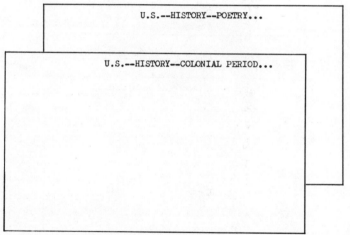

Fig. 92. Two subject added entries in prescribed order

If alphabetical order and word-by-word filing were indicated in this case we should know how to file these three blocks: Colonial<Poetry<Revolution. But at Step 5a during the fourth loop through the chart we decide that here we have a numerically filed source item. At Step 6a we transform the item "REVOLUTION" to a range of dates, perhaps "1776-1783". We perform a similar operation on the target item "COLONIAL PERIOD" at Step 6b. We mentally trans-

late that item into something like the range "1607-1776".

When we reach Step 18 we file these two entries by the numerical rank of the beginning points of the two ranges of dates,

$$1607<1776$$

or, in other words, we place the first two cards into this order:

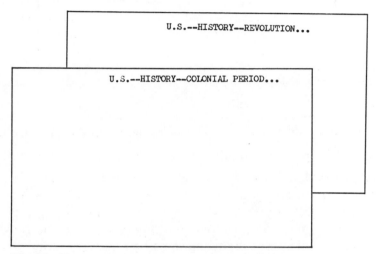

Fig. 93. Two subject added entries subarranged chronologically

When we compare the source entry with the second target entry, however, we find at Step 5b that "POETRY" is an alphabetical item. Therefore, as we compare "REVOLU-TION" with "POETRY" at Step 15, we decide that the two items ar not of the same primary ordering principle. We go to Step 16 and learn that "REVOLUTION" files anterior to "POETRY". When the three cards are in place, the file looks like this:

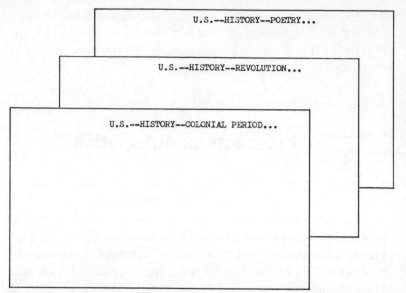

Fig. 94. Three subject added entries subarranged, chronological before alphabetical subdivisions

Undoubtedly, I could have given many more examples, working up to more and more complex filing problems. The reader may want to try a few "tough nuts" of his own choice. It will be found, however, that nothing changes in the flow of decisions that are made in the filing process. Any difficulties that arise will be found to stem from ambiguities in the criteria employed to identify blocks, sections, items, and ordering principles. Since these ambiguities are inherent in the structure of the *ALA Rules*, nothing can be done about them short of re-writing that book. Until then, filers should find the approach to the *ALA Rules* easier after a study of the underlying principles expounded above.

7. Prospects for Automation

Can a machine be made to file catalog entries? Not by the *ALA Rules* as they now stand. Or at least not if we are concerned with actual, practical filing. Granted, theoretically there is nothing in the way. Given a big enough machine and sufficient money, a team of programmers should be able, at today's state of the art, to write all the instructions necessary to do by machine what the human filer has been doing until now. But it would be a laborious program, totally impractical, certainly not a cost-effective method. Consider a set of fictitious title entries:

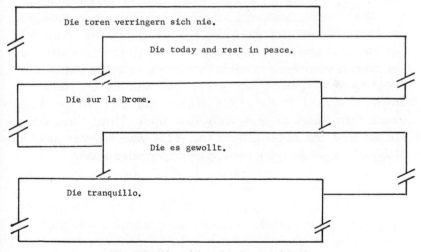

Fig. 95. Five title added entry blocks

These entries pose no particular problem to the human filer, provided he or she has the requisite liberal education. Entry 2 is in English. The first filing item is "Die". Entries 3 and 5 are in French and Latin, respectively, and the first filing items, again, are "Die" and "Die". Entries 1 and 4, of course, are in German, and although they both begin with the same configuration of letters and spaces, "Die" vs. "Die", the first item of entry 1 is a pseudo-item, while the first item of entry 4 is not. But altogether, it should have taken the filer no more than a few seconds to put these five entries into the correct order:

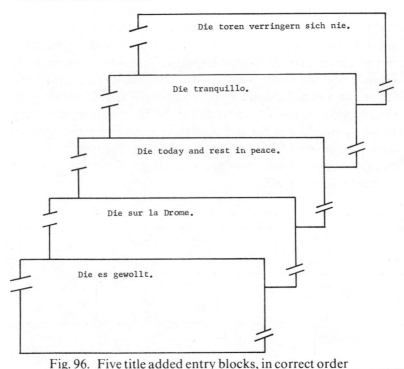

Fig. 96. Five title added entry blocks, in correct order

What about the computer, though? Who can imagine the programming required to teach the machine to distinguish between the "Die" of "Die tranquillo", on the one hand, and the "Die" of "Die toren . . ." and "Die es gewollt", on the

100

other? And how much more programming will be required to achieve the distinction between the "Die" of "Die toren . . ." (initial article) and the "Die" of "Die es gewollt" (pronoun)? How much memory will it take to store enough of the world's languages to enable the computer to make all the necessary comparisons? Will there be enough of it to store the additional network of grammatical decisions required to distinguish between such fine points as the "Die" of "Die blumen, meine freude" (initial article in the nominative case, cf. Rule 4.A.1) and the "Die" of "Die blumen zu lieben!" (initial article in the accusative case, cf. Rule 4.A.2)?

Can the machine be made to file, then? If nothing is changed—catalog entries constructed the same as always, filing rules left as they are—there is no hope. We can never automate filing in a practical way, and that is all there is to that. If, on the other hand, input to the computer were to include machine-interpretable flags for pseudo-items and similar difficulties, machine filing could be a reality very soon. But it would be a mixed blessing, at best. Consider this fictitious entry:

```
Wagner, Robert, 1900-
    A guide book to mechanics.
London, Longmans [1962]
    247p.
```

Fig. 97. Source main entry

To enable a computer to make the necessary filing decisions, a human editor would have to flag the entry in some way for card pattern, block beginnings, sections, pseudo-items, ordering principles, item transformations, substitutions, omissions, transpositions, and similar irregularities. The result might look as the entry in the following illustration.

```
!2 ¦1 Wagner,¦ Robert,¦ 1900-¦
   ¦2/A/ guide book to mechanics.¦
   London, Longmans [1962]¦
   /247p./
```

Fig. 98. "Flagged" source main entry

The entry having been thus prepared, a machine can sense the following information:

Flag	Meaning
!2	This is an entry of Pattern 2, i.e. a main entry, where the main entry block functions as author block, contains a person's name labelling a person, and the name consists of a single surname, one or more given names, and a chronological section.
¦1	Here begins the first block.
¦	Here ends a section.
¦2	Here begins the second block.
//	Between these marks is a pseudo-item.

Now let us play computer and take the Wagner entry through the flow charts of chapter 6. Before flagging, our computer would not even pass Decision 2a! For without help this extremely powerful and yet so simple-"minded" machine cannot tell the end of the first filing block, let alone the beginning of the next filing section. Using the flags provided, on the other hand, improves the situation greatly. The start of the first block is given; sections are marked;

the entry pattern is given which provides information regarding the number of sections in the block. Pseudo-items are suppressed. With this, the machine steps clear through to Decision 12.

Since the target file would be flagged in the same way—entry pattern, block numbers, section delimiters, pseudo-items, etc.—the machine would in a flash reach the pair comparison stage. Let us assume we faced this target entry:

```
¦2 ¦1 Wagner,¦ Robert,¦ 1900-¦
       ¦2 Mechanics.¦ London,
       Longmans [1969]¦
       /900p./
```

Fig. 99. "Flagged" target main entry

Here is what would happen, beginning at Decision 15:

Q. (15)	Are source and target items of the same primary ordering principle?
Ans.	Yes, since both entries are of Pattern 2.
Q. (17)	Are they alike in symbol composition?
Ans.	Yes.
Q. (19)	Is there a difference in contextual rank?
Ans.	No, since both entries are of Pattern 2.
Q. (21)	Last fileable item in source section?
Ans.	No, since Pattern 2 has three sections and this was only the first.
Q. (23)	Last fileable item this target section?
Ans.	No.
Q. (4a)	What is next source item?

etc., until the first source and target blocks have been compared and found alike.

Q. (21)	Last fileable item this source section?
Ans.	Yes, since third section end has been reached.
Q. (22)	Last fileable item this target section?
Ans.	Yes.
Q. (24)	Last section this source block?
Ans.	Yes.
Q. (25)	Last section this target block?
Ans.	Yes.
Q. (2a)	Next source block?

etc., until first source and target filing item have been reached, i.e. "guidebook" vs. "mechanics".

Q. (15)	Source and target items of same ordering principle?
Ans.	Yes, since no numerical flag was given.
Q. (17)	Source and target items alike?
Ans.	No; difference between "g" and "m".
Q. (18)	Analyse difference.
Ans.	g=7, m=13
Q. (27)	Source entry outranked by target entry?
Ans.	Yes, because 7<13, therefore g before m.
Q. (30)	Has source entry been compared to next anterior target entry?
Ans.	No; machine keeps track of steps completed.

etc., repeating until source entry comes to rest as the basic equation is fulfilled: $TE_a < SE < TE_p$.

As we can see, there is no mystery to machine filing, even by *ALA* rules. Machines are eminently capable of performing housekeeping tasks (such as remembering what block this is, how many sections there are) and ranking decisions (a before b, 6 after 5). And they can do it accurately and at electronic speeds, PROVIDED, and here is the rub, a human editor makes all the decisions that involve judgement, association, and knowledge concerning grammar, history, pronunciation, meaning, and dozens of other criteria. And that, of course, is precisely what we are trying to free ourselves from. Nothing is gained if we have to tell the computer how to file each new entry. Data processing works. But it works efficiently only for clearly defined repetitive tasks spelled out in machine-interpretable terms. Data processing bogs down when criteria are vague or ambiguous and no two successive tasks are alike.

What can be done? Undoubtedly, a compromise solution is possible. If we could live with catalogs filed strictly by the Basic Principle of the *ALA Rules*, allowing no exceptions, and if we could change entries at their birth to supress all leading pseudo-items, for example, we could have computer filing tomorrow. It is that simple. Here is what would happen. Consider again an earlier example:

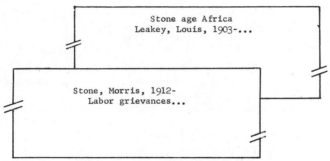

```
                    Stone age Africa
                    Leakey, Louis, 1903-...


        Stone, Morris, 1912-
           Labor grievances...
```

Fig. 100. Two entries filed by Rule 19.A.

Instead of filing a word that is a name before the same word that is not a name, a decision the machine cannot make without help, a computer filing according to the Basic Principle would file "straightforward, item by item through the entry, not disregarding or transposing any of the elements, nor mentally inserting designations". The computer would begin at the left with the "S" of Stone, then compare the t's, the o's, etc. until the first difference is reached (comma in the author main entry block versus space in the title added entry block). Assuming that "space" files before "comma", the new order is shown in the next example.

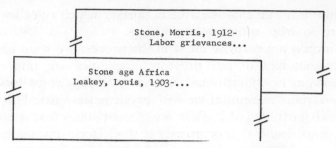

Fig. 101. Two entries filed according to the Basic
Principle (*ALA Rules*, p.1)

What shall we say, then? What *are* the prospects for automation? It all depends on what librarians and their public
are willing to sacrifice. If we insist on the 300-plus distinctions between entries made by the *ALA Rules*, then the out-
look is hopeless. That is a safe statement. If we can tolerate
the collating sequence of the computer without changes,
automation is here already. There can be no doubt about
that, either. Between these two extremes we must seek our
compromise.

The next move, it seems, belongs to the library profession.
What is required is a thorough reappraisal of the objectives
of our filing rules, a good look at the desired output of the
filing process. Is it necessary to collect all "Baghdad" entries
together even if they are spelled differently? Do we have to
unite McDonald with MacDonald? Must we file 5, 4, 6
instead of 4, 5, 6? On the basis of what research did the compilers of the *ALA Rules* deem it "more practical from the
point of view of use" to deviate from alphabetical order as
often as they did? (cf. Rule 19) Which principle leads to
easier catalog use, "the alphabet . . . uniform order . . .
that can be easily understood" (*ALA Rules*, p.vi); "arrangement . . . how they are spoken" (*ALA Rules*, p. 13); or
"arrange . . . because . . . identical in meaning" (*ALA
Rules*, p. 74). In other words, do people look for words as
written, as spoken, or by their meaning? Once we determine
precisely what we need in output oriented terms, i.e. how
users get information out of the catalog, not how librarians

106

can put it in, we shall be able to specify which rules we can afford to drop, which we must keep.

It would not surprise me if in the process we were to discover that half of our present filing rules are imprecise, redundant, or superfluous. For an example, let us look at Rule 4 from the point of view of a systems designer. This rule has two parts, A and B. Part A expressly states that it covers initial articles. But how precise is this? Does this really tell us enough? What is an initial article, for example? Since the *ALA Rules* fails to define this term we must assume that it is common knowledge. Perhaps the dictionary definition of "initial" helps:

> *initial*, adj. (2) placed or standing at the beginning (the ~ word of a verse)

An initial article, then, might be defined as an article that stands at the beginning. At the beginning of what, we must ask. This is not explained in Rule 4.A and it is for such lack of precision, among other things, that the *ALA Rules* cannot be automated as they stand. A computer cannot do anything with Rule 4.A unless it is given clear, unambiguous definitions. Actually, the human filer must also know. But we tacitly assume that the human filer is "intelligent" enough to supply his own answers in such cases. As a matter of fact, our human filer will probably assume that an initial article is an article that stands at the beginning of a heading or block. In the added entry block

The beauty and the beast

he recognizes the "the" of beauty as an initial article, and the "the" of beast an a non-initial article.

Having determined, at least tentatively, what this initial article of Rule 4.A is, let us look at 4.B. The logic of classification requires that if Rule 4 deals with articles, is divided into A and B, and A deals with initial articles, then 4.B *must* deal with non-initial articles. And it does. Rule 4.B has this scope note: "Articles within the entry". The careful reader may have noticed that Rule 4.B supplies the information we needed a moment ago to answer the question: "At the beginning of what?" For by the requirements of logic, if articles are divided into two groups, A and B, and B covers those *within* the entry, than A, dealing with initial articles, *must* cover those *at the beginning* of the entry.

The *ALA Rules*, having been compiled before the computer forced us to think logically, completely muddled this point by failing to define "entry" in any definitive way, as we have observed elsewhere. If we read the rest of Rule 4.B, we can see that "entry" here is taken in sense 2 of the Glossary, as the equivalent of "heading".

At this point we recognize, then, that Rule 4.A deals with articles at the beginning of a title or a heading, while Rule 4.B deals with articles within a title or a heading. But is this last rule not redundant? If there are only two kinds of articles, initial articles and those within headings, and if we have a rule (4.A) that directs us to disregard initial articles, it follows that the only possible other kind of article is to be regarded—we do not need a special rule for that. If a coin has two sides, Heads and Tails, and we flip it, and it lands Heads up, we do not need an investigation to determine what is on the other side. We already know! Therefore, we do not need Rule 4.B—unless there is another kind of article that has been kept secret so far. And that, it seems, is what happened. Rule 4.B actually smuggles in two more kinds of articles, the "initial" article in an inverted position ("at the beginning of what?", we ask again), and the initial article at the beginning of a subdivision (notice how that differs from "title or heading"). What emerges are four rules, not two:

4.A. Disregard articles at the beginning of a title or heading.
4.B. Regard articles within a title or a heading.
(4.C) Disregard articles in an inverted position.
(4.D) Disregard articles at the beginning of a sub-division.

To clean this up we only have to combine the three "disregard" rules and abolish the superfluous Rule 4.B. The result of such a simplification might be

Rule 4. ARTICLES
Disregard all articles at the beginning of titles, headings, and subdivisions; also all articles in an inverted position. Regard all other articles.

We need not take time to discuss the rest of Rule 4 which has many other hidden inconsistencies built into its structure, not to speak of almost a dozen stated exceptions, notably Rules 14, 15.A.1, 17, 5, 12.A, 14.F, 15.A.5, 27C.1, 37.B.5, 37.B.6, and 33.E.

We need not discuss Rule 6 which directs filers to treat abbreviations now "as if spelled in full" (6.A.1), now "as if written in full" (6.B), and then again "as they are written, not as if spelled in full" (6.C), causing one to suspect that what really happens is none too clear. Or Rules 1.C, 2.A.2, 6.A.2, 15.A.3, and others which are not even filing rules but suggestions for catalogers. And it probably will not pay us to wonder at this point why we need so many "Basic Rules" and statements of "Basic Order" (notably on pages 2, 55, 114, 121, 134, 155, 165, 174, and 218) when we were already given a "Basic Principle" and a "Basic Order" on page 1. Nor can we justify here an investigation into the chain of reasons by which the framers of the *ALA Rules* came to include directions for the treatment of Anglo-Saxon, Icelandic, and Turkish letters among the first four "basic" rules.

The point, I think, is clear: our present rules are not a suitable starting point. If we seriously want to consider automation we must begin with a thorough analysis of our entire system of cataloging and filing rules. We must lay our rules out in a well-defined, unambiguous, logical flow pattern that leads to a catalog arrangement that fulfills the objectives set for it.

But what if, perish the thought, we should find that even

after careful rewriting, the rules and decision are too complex for the unaided computer? The exercise would still have been worth the trouble: imagine a humanly readable book of filing rules!

Part II

8. First Aid Guide for Practical Filing

The First Aid Guide that follows is an attempt to reduce library catalog card filing to a set of decisions that can be made on the basis of clear, visible distinctions in the structure of catalog cards. This is in contrast to the *ALA Rules* which rely heavily on abstract decision criteria which are seldom adequately defined. For example, Rule 31.C prescribes the order for "different kinds of entries under the same heading". In as much as the Glossary offers three different definitions for the term "entry", but Rule 31.C does not specify which definition applies, it requires considerable effort to interpret this rule. In sense 2 of the Glossary, "heading", for example, is synonymous with "entry", but it is unlikely that the compilers of the *ALA Rules* should have meant to say "different headings under the same heading". The term "entry" here then must either mean "record of a bibliographical entity" in sense 1 of the Glossary, or "title" in sense 3 of the Glossary (which, to complicate matters further, was given but not numbered).

Now, if the filer decides at this point to accept the third definition, the rule must be interpreted to apply to "different kinds of titles in cards for works entered under title that have identical headings". This can hardly have been the intended meaning since under (1) immediately below there is mention of author main entries having precedence over certain other entries. The only remaining interpretation of

Rule 31.C is that it applies to "different records of bibliographic entities that have identical headings". While it is possible for two cards to have identical headings, even identical geographical name headings, it is not possible for these two identical headings to be different in kind as they would have to be under Rule 31.C., which distributes them into different groups by author, subject, title, etc. The filer is left with an insoluble logical dilemma: to arrange two things that are alike by their differences!

Such puzzles abound in the *ALA Rules*. The First Aid Guide presented here attempts a fresh start: all decisions are based on concrete, observable characteristics of actual catalog cards, as was stated above. Also, since all filing ultimately reduces to the comparison of two entries, two cards, at a time, only pair comparisons are covered by the instructions of the Guide.

If we consider that library catalog cards come in a great variety of block configurations—main entries, added entries; one section, several sections; given names, surnames, and fictitious names, labelling persons or corporate entities; authorship information, title information, or subject information—we shall not be surprised to learn that the number of pairs of entries that differ in aspects that are critical to filing reaches into the hundreds, if not thousands. In an attempt to reduce this Guide to feasible proportions I have selected twenty-one patterns of cards that I believe to occur most often in practical filing. Included in this section are ten main entry card patterns distinguished from each other by differences in the structure, function, and contents of the main entry block, and eleven added entry card patterns distinguished from each other by differences in the added entry block. Only cards with one added entry block have been selected. Cards with more than one added entry block have been excluded from the Guide.

The Guide consists of two parts, a Pattern Identification Section and a Permutation Section. In the Pattern Identification Section are listed the twenty-one selected card patterns, with an example for each. To use the Guide, the filer selects one card to be filed, and one card from the catalog into which he is filing, preferably a potential neighbour of the card to be filed. For each card in the resulting pair the pattern number is determined from the Pattern Identification Section.

Here is an example. Let us say we wished to file this entry:

```
Stone, Morris, 1912-
    Labor grievances and decisions.
New York, American Arbitration
Association, 1970.
    220p.
```

Fig. 102. Author main entry

into a catalog that contained the following card as a potential neighbour:

```
Stone age Africa

Leakey, Louis, 1903-
    Stone age Africa.  New York,
Negro Universities Press, 1970.
    218p.
```

Fig. 103. Title added entry

The first entry is readily identified as a main entry. The main entry block is fairly typical: it functions as author block and contains a single surname, a given name, and a date. The Pattern Identification Section assigns to this card pattern the number 2.

The second card is an added entry with one added entry block functioning as title block. It contains a natural title. According to the Pattern Identification Section this is a card of pattern 15.

The filer now turns to the Permutation Section where all possible combinations of the twenty-one card patterns paired with themselves and with each other—a total of 231 permutations—have been considered. Under 2:15 (the pattern numbers of the two cards in the pair used as an example, lowest number first) the filer is asked to compare the first items, in this case "Stone" and "Stone". Obviously, the two items are alike. Based on this unambiguous criterion the decision is to file the card of pattern 2 before the one of pattern 15, or thus:

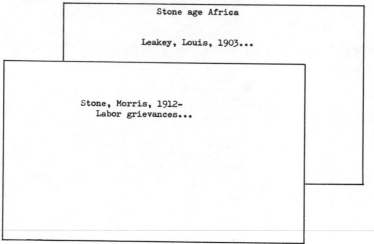

Fig. 104. Two entries filed by Rule 19.A.

To support the preceding instruction, an ALA rule number is cited, in this case Rule 19.A. Inspection of that rule will confirm that the example given can be identified in terms of the *ALA Rules* as a pair of cards with the same word "used as the heading" for two "different kinds of entry", and that the order prescribed by the *ALA Rules* is identical to the order derived from the Guide.

As I have pointed out above, the Guide is limited to 231 permutations of 21 patterns. The filing order of other card patterns must be determined either by applying the *ALA Rules* or the general decision charts presented in chapter 6.

First Aid Guide for Practical Filing

I. Pattern Identification Section

MAIN ENTRY

Main entry block functions as author block

Main entry block contains a person's name labelling a person

Person's name consists of a single surname and one or more given names:

1

```
Hatch, Elvin J.
    Theories of man and culture.
New York, Columbia University Press,
1973.
    384p.
```

Person's name consists of a single surname, one or more given names, and a chronological section:

2

```
Heiliger, Edward M., 1909-
    Library automation: experience,
methodology and technology.  New
York, McGraw-Hill, 1971.
    333p.
```

Person's name consists of a single surname,
one or more given names, and a title of address:

3

```
Hardy, Sir Alister Clavering
    The open sea, its natural history.
Boston, Houghton Mifflin, 1956.
```

Person's name consists of a compound surname
and one or more given names:

4

```
Lloyd George, David
    Family letters, 1885-1936.  Oxford
University Press, 1973.
```

*Main entry block contains a person's name labelling
a corporate entity:*

5

```
Wilson, H. W., firm, publishers
    Standard catalog for high school
libraries; a selected catalog...
New York, 1928-
```

*Main entry block contains a fictitious name label-
ling a corporate entity*
Fictitious name
Fictitious name not further subdivided:

6

```
Field and stream
    The field and stream game bag.
Garden City, New York, Doubleday,
1948.
```

Fictitious name consists of one name and
one or more subdivisions:

7

```
California.  University.  University
        at Los Angeles.  Real Estate
        Research Program.
    Industrial location bibliography.
Los Angeles, 1959.
    82 l.
```

Fictitious name consists of one name and a
uniform title:

8

```
California.  Laws, statutes, etc.
    Health and safety code annotated
of the State of California.  San
Francisco, Bancroft-Whitney Co.,
1961.
        4 v.
```

Main entry block functions as title block
Main entry block contains a natural title:

9

> New American plays. Edited and
> with an introduction by Robert
> W. Corrigan. New York, Hill
> and Wanford, 1965-

Main entry block contains a uniform title:

10

> Bible. English. 1961.
> The new English Bible. New
> York, Oxford University Press,
> 1961-

ADDED ENTRY*
Added entry block functions as author block
Added entry block contains a person's name
Person's name consists of a single surname,
one or more given names, and a designation
indicating relationship of author to work, over
an author main entry:

11

> Heimer, Ralph T., jt. auth.
>
> Nichols, Eugene Douglas.
> Algebra... New York, Holt,
> Rinehart and Winston, 1966.
> 582p.

*In contrast to the definition of the *ALA Rules*, this guide considers as added
entries all cards that are not main entries.

Person's name consists of a single surname, one or more given names, and a designation indicating relationship of author to work, over a title main entry:

12

```
Hart, Pembroke J., ed.


The earth's crust;  structure, dynamic
   processes, and... Washington, D.C.,
   Geophysical Union, 1969.
```

Added entry block contains a fictitious name labelling a corporate entity, over an author main entry:

13

```
Washington Post


Ehrlich, Paul, comp.
   Famous firsts; readings from
the Washington Post...  San Francisco,
Fryman, 1971.
```

Added entry block contains a fictitious name labelling a corporate entity, over a title main entry:

14

```
Scientific American


From cell to organism;  readings from
   the Scientific American...  San
   Francisco, Freeman, 1967.
   256p.
```

Added entry block functions as title block
Added entry block contains a natural title:

15

```
        Marianne Moore


   Tomlinson, Charles, 1927-    comp.
      Marianne Moore; a collection of
   critical essays.  Englewood Cliffs,
   N.J., Prentice-Hall, 1968.
      185p.
```

Added entry block functions as subject block
Added entry block contains a single one-word subject heading:

16

```
            AGING


   Jonas, David
      Young till we die...  New York,
   Coward, McCann, 1973.
```

Added entry block contains a single multi-word subject heading:

17

```
         ARCHITECTURE, ITALIAN


   Wolfflin, Heinrich, 1864-1945.
      Renaissance and baroque...
   Ithaca, Ny.Y., Cornell University
   Press, 1966.
      183p.
```

Added entry block contains a subject heading and an alphabetical subdivision:

18

```
        NETHERLANDS--DESCRIPTION AND TRAVEL


    Holland.  New York, D. McKay
        v.
```

Added entry block contains a subject heading and a chronological subdivision:

19

```
        DRAMA--20TH CENTURY



    King, Woodie, comp.
        Black drama anthology.  New York,
    Columbia University Press, 1972.
```

Added entry block contains a person's name:

20

```
        SANGER, MARGARET, 1879-1966


    Dash, Joan
        A life of one's own...  New York,
    Harper and Row, 1974.
        388p.
```

Added entry block contains an author's name and a title:

21

SHAKESPEARE, WILLIAM, 1564–1616––HAMLET

Joseph, Bertram Leon.
    Conscience and the King.   London
Chatto and Windus, 1953.
    175p.

II. Permutation Section

Pattern Pair	Conditions (if any)	Instructions	Applicable ALA rule Number
1:1	If first blocks are alike	File by first different filing element in the title	1.B
	If only the leading sections are alike	File by first different filing element in the given name section	1.B
	If leading sections are unlike	File by first different filing element in the first block	1.B
1:2	If leading and given name sections are alike	File Pattern 1 before Pattern 2	20.E.1
	If only the leading sections are alike	File by first different filing element in the given name section	1.B
	If leading sections are unlike	File by first different filing element in the block	1.B
1:3	If leading and given name sections are alike	File Pattern 1 before Pattern 3	20.E.2

Pattern Pair	Conditions (if any)	Instructions	Applicable ALA rule Number
	If only the leading sections are alike	File by first different filing element in the second section	20.D.1
	If leading sections are unlike	File by first different filing element in the first block	1.B
1:4	If first items are alike	File Pattern 1 before Pattern 4	21.A
	If first items are unlike	File by first different filing element in the first block	1.B
1:5	If leading and given name sections are alike	File Pattern 1 before Pattern 5	23.A.2
	If only the leading sections are alike	File by first different filing element in the given name section	23.A.1
1:6	If first items are alike	File Pattern 1 before Pattern 6	19.A

Pattern Pair	Conditions (if any)	Instructions	Applicable ALA rule Number
	If first items are unlike	File by first different filing element in the first block	1.B
1:7	If first items are alike	File Pattern 1 before Pattern 7	19.A
	If first items are unlike	File by first different filing element in the first block	1.B
1:8	If first items are alike	File Pattern 1 before Pattern 8	19.A
	If first items are unlike	File by first different filing element in the first block	1.B
1:9	If first items are alike	File Pattern 1 before Pattern 9	19.A
	If first items are unlike	File by first different filing element in the first block	1.B

Pattern Pair	Conditions (if any)	Instructions	Applicable ALA rule Number
1:10	If first items are alike	File Pattern 1 before Pattern 10	29.A
	If first items are unlike	File by first different filing element in the first block	1.B
1:11	If leading and given name sections are alike	File by first different filing element in the title, ignoring designation	26.B.2 20.A.3 26.B.3
	If only the leading sections are alike	File by first different filing element in the given name section	19.A.1)
	If leading sections are unlike	File by first different filing element in the first block	1.B
1:12	If leading and given name sections are alike	File by first different filing element in the title, ignoring designation	26.B.2 20.A.3 26.B.3

Pattern Pair	Conditions (if any)	Instructions	Applicable ALA rule Number
	If only the leading sections are alike	File by first different filing element in the given name section	19.A.1)
	If leading sections arc unlike	File by first different filing element in the first block	1.B
1:13	If first items are alike	File Pattern 1 before Pattern 13	19.A
	If first items are unlike	File by first different filing element in the first block	1.B
1:14	If first items alike	File Pattern 1 before Pattern 14	19.A
	If first items are unlike	File by first different filing element in the first block	1.B
1:15	If first items are alike	File Pattern 1 before Pattern 15	19.A

Pattern Pair	Conditions (if any)	Instructions	Applicable ALA rule Number
	If first items are unlike	File by first different filing element in the first block	1.B
1:16	If first items are alike	File Pattern 1 before Pattern 16	19.A
	If first items are unlike	File by first different filing element in the first block	1.B
1:17	If first items are alike	File Pattern 1 before Pattern 17	19.A
	If first items are unlike	File by first different filing element in the first block	1.B
1:18	If first items are alike	File Pattern 1 before Pattern 18	19.A
	If first items are unlike	File by first different filing element in the first block	1.B

Pattern Pair	Conditions (if any)	Instructions	Applicable ALA rule Number
1:19	If first items are alike	File Pattern 1 before Pattern 19	19.A
	If first items are unlike	File by first different filing element in the first block	1.B
1:20	If leading and given name sections are alike	File Pattern 1 before Pattern 20	19.B.1
	If only the leading sections are alike	File by first different filing element in the given name section	1.B
	If leading sections are unlike	File by first different filing element in the first block	1.B
1:21	If leading and given name sections are alike	File Pattern 1 before Pattern 21	19.B.1
	If only the leading sections are alike	File by first different filing element in the given name section	1.B

Pattern Pair	Conditions (if any)	Instructions	Applicable ALA rule Number
	If leading sections are unlike	File by first different filing element in the first block	1.B
2:2	If first blocks are alike	File by first different filing element in the title	1.B
	If chronological sections only are unlike	File by numerical rank of chronological section	20.E.3
	If only the leading sections are alike	File by first different filing element in the given name section	1.B
	If leading sections are unlike	File by first different filing element in the first block	1.B
2:3	If leading and given name sections are alike	File Pattern 2 before Pattern 3	20.E.1.2)
	If only the leading sections are alike	File by first different filing element in the given name section, ignoring designation	1.B 20.D.3

133

Pattern Pair	Conditions (if any)	Instructions	Applicable ALA rule Number
	If leading sections are unlike	File by first different filing element in the first block	1.B
2:4	If first items are alike	File Pattern 2 before Pattern 4	21.A
	If first items are unlike	File by first different filing element in the first block	1.B
2:5	If leading and given name sections are alike	File Pattern 2 before Pattern 5	23.A.2
	If only the leading sections are alike	File by first different filing element in the given name section	1.B
	If leading sections are unlike	File by first different filing element in the first block	1.B
2:6 through 2:10	If first items are alike	File Pattern 2 before Patterns 6 through 10, respectively	19.A

Pattern Pair	Conditions (if any)	Instructions	Applicable ALA rule Number
	If first items are unlike	File by first different filing element in the first block	1.B
2:11	If leading and given name sections are alike	File Pattern 2 before Pattern 11, ignoring designation	20.E.1 20.A.3 26.B.3
	If only the leading sections are alike	File by first different filing element in the given name section	1.B
	If leading sections are unlike	File by first different filing element in the first block	1.B
2:12	If leading and given name sections are alike	File Pattern 12 before Pattern 2, ignoring designation	20.E.1 20.A.3 26.B.3
	If only the leading sections are alike	File by first different filing element in the given name section	1.B
	If leading sections are unlike	File by first different filing element in the first block	1.B

Pattern Pair	Conditions (if any)	Instructions	Applicable ALA rule Number
2:13 through 2:19	If first items are alike	File Pattern 2 before Patterns 13 through 19, respectively	19.A
	If first items are unlike	File by first different filing element in the first block	1.B
2:20	If first blocks are alike	File Pattern 2 before Pattern 20	19.B.1
	If chronological sections only are unlike	File by numerical rank of chronological section	20.E.3
	If only the leading sections are alike	File by first different filing element in the given name section	1.B
	If leading sections are unlike	File by first different filing element in the first block	1.B
2:21	If leading sections, given name sections, and chronological sections are alike	File by first different filing element in the title	26.B.12

Pattern Pair	Conditions (if any)	Instructions	Applicable ALA rule Number
	If chronological sections only are unlike	File by numerical rank of chronological section	20.E.3
	If only the leading sections are alike	File by first different filing element in the given name section	1.B
	If leading sections are unlike	File by first different filing element in the first block	1.B
3:3	If first blocks are alike	File by first different filing element in the title	1.B
	If leading and given name sections are alike	File by first different filing element of the designation	20.E.2
	If only the leading sections are alike	File by first different filing element in the given name section	1.B
	If leading sections are unlike	File by first different filing element in the first block	1.B

Pattern Pair	Conditions (if any)	Instructions	Applicable ALA rule Number
3:4	If first items are alike	File Pattern 3 before Pattern 4	21.A
	If first items are unlike	File by first different filing element in the first block	1.B
3:5	If leading and given name sections are alike	File by first different filing element in the remaining part of the block	23.A.1
	If only the leading sections are alike	File by first different filing element in the given name section	1.B
	If leading sections are unlike	File by first different filing element in the first block	1.B
3:6 through 3:10	If first items are alike	File Pattern 3 before Patterns 6 through 10, respectively	19.A
	If first items are unlike	File by first different filing element in the first block	1.B

Pattern Pair	Conditions (if any)	Instructions	Applicable ALA rule Number
3:11 and 3:12	If first blocks are alike	File by first different filing element in the title	26.B.2
	If leading and given name sections are alike	File Pattern 11 before Pattern 3, ignoring designation	20.E.1 20.A.3 26.B.3
	If only the leading sections are alike	File by first different filing element in the given name section	1.B
	If leading sections are unlike	File by first different filing element in the first block	1.B
3:13 through 3:19	If first items are alike	File Pattern 3 before Patterns 13 through 19, respectively	19.A
	If first items are unlike	File by first different filing element in the first block	1.B
3:20	If leading and given name sections are alike	File Pattern 3 before Pattern 20	20.E.1

Pattern Pair	Conditions (if any)	Instructions	Applicable ALA rule Number
	If only the leading sections are alike	File by first different filing element in the given name section	1.B
	If leading sections are unlike	File by first different filing element in the first block	1.B
3:21	If leading and given name sections are alike	File Pattern 3 before Pattern 21	20.E.1
	If only the leading sections are alike	File by first different filing element in the given name section	1.B
	If leading sections are unlike	File by first different filing element in the first block	1.B
4:4	If first blocks are alike	File by first different filing element in the title	1.B
	If only the leading sections are alike	File by first different filing element in the given name section	1.B

Pattern Pair	Conditions (if any)	Instructions	Applicable ALA rule Number
	If leading sections are unlike	File by first different filing element in the first block	1.B
4:5	If first items are alike	File Pattern 5 before Pattern 4	21.A
	If first items are unlike	File by first different filing element in the first block	1.B
4:6 through 4:10	no special conditions	File by first different filing element in the first block	1.B
4:11 through 4:19	If first items are alike	File Patterns 11 through 19, respectively, before Pattern 4	19, 21.A
	If first items are unlike	File by first different filing element in the first block	1.B
4:20	If first items are alike	File Pattern 20 before Pattern 4	19.B.1

Pattern Pair	Conditions (if any)	Instructions	Applicable ALA rule Number
	If first items are unlike	File by first different filing element in the first block	1.B
4:21	If first items are alike	File Pattern 21 before Pattern 4	19.B
	If first items are unlike	File by first different filing element in the first block	1.B
5:5	If first blocks are alike	File by first different filing element in the title	1.B
	If leading and given name sections are alike	File by first different filing element in the remaining part of the block	23.A.1
	If only the leading sections are alike	File by first different filing element in the given name section	1.B
	If leading sections are unlike	File by first different filing element in the first block	1.B

Pattern Pair	Conditions (if any)	Instructions	Applicable ALA rule Number
5:6	If first items are alike	File Pattern 5 before Pattern 6	19.A
	If first items are unlike	File by first different filing element in the first block	1.B
5:7 through 5:10	If first items are alike	File Pattern 5 before Patterns 7 through 10, respectively	23.A.1
	If first items are unlike	File by first different filing element in the first block	1.B
5:11 and 5:12	If leading and given name sections are alike	File Pattern 11 before Pattern 5, ignoring designation	20.E.1 20.A.3
	If only the leading sections are alike	File by first different filing element in the given name section	1.B
	If leading sections are unlike	File by first different filing element in the first block	1.B

Pattern Pair	Conditions (if any)	Instructions[1]	Applicable ALA rule Number
5:13 through 5:19	If first items are alike	File Pattern 5 before Patterns 13 through 19, respectively	19.A
	If first items are unlike	File by first different filing element in the first block	1.B
5:20	If leading and given name sections are alike	File Pattern 5 before Pattern 20	19.B.1
	If only the leading sections are alike	File by first different filing element in the given name section	1.B
	If leading sections are unlike	File by first different filing element in the first block	1.B
5:21	If leading and given name sections are alike	File Pattern 5 before Pattern 21	19.B.1
	If only the leading sections are alike	File by first different filing element in the given name section	1.B

Pattern Pair	Conditions (if any)	Instructions	Applicable ALA rule Number
	If leading sections are unlike	File by first different filing element in the first block	1.B
6:6	If first blocks are alike	File by first different filing element in the title	1.B
	If first blocks are unlike	File by first different filing element in the first block	1.B
6:7 and 6:8	no special conditions	File by first different filing element in the first block	1.B
6:9 and 6:10	If only the leading sections are alike	File Pattern 6 before Patterns 9 and 10, respectively	33.C
	If leading sections are unlike	File by first different filing element in the first block	1.B
6:11	If first items are alike	File Pattern 6 before Pattern 11	19.A

Pattern Pair	Conditions (if any)	Instructions	Applicable ALA rule Number
	If first items are unlike	File by first different filing element in the first block	1.B
6:12	If first items are alike	File Pattern 6 before Pattern 12	19.A
	If first items are unlike	File by first different filing element in the first block	1.B
6:13 and 6:14	If first blocks are alike	File by first different filing element in the title	26.B.2
	If first blocks are unlike	File by first different filing element in the first block	1.B
6:15	If first blocks are alike	File by first different filing element of next block	28.A
	If first blocks are unlike	File by first different filing element in the first block	1.B

Pattern Pair	Conditions (if any)	Instructions	Applicable ALA rule Number
6:16 and 6:17	If first blocks are alike	File Pattern 6 before Patterns 16 and 17, respectively	28.C
	If first blocks are unlike	File by first different filing element in the first block	1.B
6:18 and 6:19	If only the leading sections are alike	File Pattern 6 before Patterns 18 and 19, respectively	28.C
	If leading sections are unlike	File by first different filing element in the first block	1.B
6:20 and 6:21	If only the leading sections are alike	File Pattern 20 and 21, respectively, before Pattern 6	19.A
	If leading sections are unlike	File by first different filing element in the first block	1.B
7:7	If first blocks are alike	File by first different filing element in the title	1.B

Pattern Pair	Conditions (if any)	Instructions	Applicable ALA rule Number
	If first blocks are unlike	File by first different filing element in the first block	1.B
7:8	If only the leading sections are alike	File by first different filing element in the second section	1.B
	If leading sections are unlike	File by first different filing element in the first block	1.B
7:9 and 7:10	no special conditions	File by first different filing element in the first block	28.A
7:11 and 7:12	If first items are alike	File Pattern 11 and 12, respectively, before Pattern 7	19.A
	If first items are unlike	File by first different filing element in the first block	1.B
7:13	no special conditions	File by first different filing element in the first block	31.B

Pattern Pair	Conditions (if any)	Instructions	Applicable ALA rule Number
7:14	If first blocks are alike	File by first different filing element in the title	1.B
	If first blocks are unlike	File by first different filing element in the first block	1.B
7:15 through 7:17	If first blocks are alike	File by first different filing element of next block	28.A
	If first blocks are unlike	File by first different filing element in the first block	1.B
7:18 and 7:19	no special conditions	File by first different filing element in the first block	28.C
7:20 and 7:21	If first items are alike	File Pattern 20 and 21 respectively, before Pattern 7	19.A
	If first items are unlike	File by first different filing element in the first block	1.B

Pattern Pair	Conditions (if any)	Instructions	Applicable ALA rule Number
8:8	If first blocks are alike	File by first different filing element of next block	1.B
	If first blocks are unlike	File by first different filing element in the first block	1.B
8:9	If first items are alike	File Pattern 8 before Pattern 9	31.C
	If first items are unlike	File by first different filing element in the first block	1.B
8:10	If only the leading sections are alike	File Pattern 8 before Pattern 10	31.C
	If leading sections are unlike	File by first different filing element in the first block	1.B
8:11 and 8:12	If first items are alike	File Patterns 11 and 12, respectively, before Pattern 8	19.A

Pattern Pair	Conditions (if any)	Instructions	Applicable ALA rule Number
	If first items are unlike	File by first different filing element in the first block	1.B
8:13	no special conditions	File by first different filing element in the first block	31.B
8:14 and 8:15	no special conditions	File by first different filing element in the first block	28.A
8:16	If first blocks are alike	File Pattern 8 before Pattern 16	28.C
	If first blocks are unlike	File by first different filing element in the first block	1.B
8:17	If first items are alike	File Pattern 8 before Pattern 17	28.C
	If first items are unlike	File by first different filing element in the first block	1.B

Pattern Pair	Conditions (if any)	Instructions	Applicable ALA rule Number
8:18	no special conditions	File by first different filing element in the first block	31.B
8:19	no special conditions	File by first different filing element in the first block	28.C
8:20 and 8:21	If first items are alike	File Patterns 20 and 21, respectively, before Pattern 8	19.A
	if first items are unlike	File by first different filing element in the first block	1.B
9:9	no special conditions	File by first different filing element in the first block	1.B
9:10	no special conditions	File by first different filing element in the first block	29.B
9:11 and 9:12	If first items are alike	File Patterns 11 and 12, respectively, before Pattern 9	19.A

Pattern Pair	Conditions (if any)	Instructions	Applicable ALA rule Number
	If first items are unlike	File by first different filing element in the first block	1.B
9:13 and 9:14	no special conditions	File by first different filing element in the first block	28.A
9:15 through 9:19	no special conditions	File by first different filing element in the first block	1.B
9:20 and 9:21	If first items are alike	File Patterns 20 and 21, respectively, before Pattern 9	19.A
	If first items are unlike	File by first different filing element in the first block	1.B
10:10	If first blocks are alike	File by first different filing element in the title	1.B
	If chronological sections only are unlike	File by numerical rank of chronological section	29.C

Pattern Pair	Conditions (if any)	Instructions	Applicable ALA rule Number
	If only the leading sections are alike	File by first different filing element in the remaining part of the block	1.B
	If leading sections are unlike	File by first different filing element in the first block	29.B
10:11 and 10:12	If first items are alike	File Patterns 11 and 12, respectively, before Pattern 10	19.A
	If first items are unlike	File by first different filing element in the first block	1.B
10:13 through 10:19	no special conditions	File by first different filing element in the first block	29.B
10:20 and 10:21	If first items are alike	File Patterns 20 and 21, respectively, before Pattern 10	29.A
	If first items are unlike	File by first different filing element of first block	1.B

Pattern Pair	Conditions (if any)	Instructions	Applicable ALA rule Number
11:11 and 11:12	If first blocks are alike	File by first different filing element in the title	26.B.2
	If leading and given name sections are alike	File by first different filing element in the title	26.B.2 20.A.3
	If only the leading sections are alike	File by first different filing element in the given name section	19.A.1)
	If leading sections are unlike	File by first different filing element in the first block	1.B
11:13 through 11:19	If first items are alike	File Patterns 13 through 19, respectively, before Pattern 11	19.A
	If first items are unlike	File by first different filing element in the first block	1.B
11:20	If leading and given name sections are alike	File Pattern 11 before Pattern 20	19.B.1

Pattern Pair	Conditions (if any)	Instructions	Applicable ALA rule Number
	If only the leading sections are alike	File by first different filing element in the given name section	19.A.1
	If leading sections are unlike	File by first different filing element in the first block	1.B
11:21	If leading and given name sections are alike	File Pattern 11 before Pattern 21	20.E.1
	If only the leading sections are alike	File by first different filing element in the given name section	19.A.1
	If leading sections are unlike	File by first different filing element in the first block	1.B
12:12	If leading and given name sections are alike	File by first different filing element in the title	26.B.2 20.A.3
	If only the leading sections are alike	File by first different filing element in the given name section	19.A.1)

Pattern Pair	Conditions (if any)	Instructions	Applicable ALA rule Number
	If leading sections are unlike	File by first different filing element in the first block	1.B
12:13 through 12:19	If first items are alike	File Patterns 13 through 19, respectively, before Pattern 12	19.A
	If first items are unlike	File by first different filing element in the first block	1.B
12:20 and 12:21	If leading and given name sections are alike	File Pattern 12 before Patterns 20 and 21, respectively	20.E.1
	If only the leading sections are alike	File by first different filing element in the given name section	19.A.1)
	If leading sections are unlike	File by first different filing element in the first block	1.B
13:13 and 13:14	If first blocks are alike	File by first different filing element in the title	26.B.2

Pattern Pair	Conditions (if any)	Instructions	Applicable ALA rule Number
	If first blocks are unlike	File by first different filing element in the first block	1.B
13:15	no special conditions	File by first different filing element in the first block	28.A
13:16 through 13:19	no special conditions	File by first different filing element in the first block	28.C
13:20 and 13:21	If first items are alike	Filing Patterns 20 and 21 respectively, before Pattern 13	19.A
	If first items are unlike	File by first different filing element in the first block	1.B
14:14	If first blocks are alike	File by first different filing element in the title	1.B
	If first blocks are unlike	File by first different filing element in the first block	1.B

Pattern Pair	Conditions (if any)	Instructions	Applicable ALA rule Number
14:15	If first blocks are alike	File by first different filing element of next block	1.B
	If first blocks are unlike	File by first different filing element in the first block	28.A
14:16 and 14:17	If the first blocks are alike	File by first different filing element of next block	1.B
	If first blocks are unlike	File by first different filing element in the first block	28.C
14:18 and 14:19	No special conditions	File by first different filing element in the first block	28.C
14:20 and 14:21	If first items are alike	File Patterns 20 and 21, respectively, before Pattern 14	19.A
	If first items are unlike	File by first different filing element in the first block	28.C

Pattern Pair	Conditions (if any)	Instructions	Applicable ALA rule Number
15:15	If first blocks are alike	File by first different filing element of next block	1.B
	If first blocks are unlike	File by first different filing element in the first block	1.B
15:16 through 15:19	no special conditions	File by first different filing element in the first block	1.B
15:20 and 15:21	If first items are alike	File Patterns 20 and 21, respectively, before Pattern 15	19.A
	If first items are unlike	File by first different filing element in the first block	1.B
16:16	If first blocks are alike	File by first different filing element of next block	1.B
	If first blocks are unlike	File by first different filing element in the first block	1.B

Pattern Pair	Conditions (if any)	Instructions	Applicable ALA rule Number
16:17 through 16:19	If first items are alike	File Patterns 16 before Patterns 17 through 19, respectively	1.B
	If first items are unlike	File by first different filing element in the first block	1.B
16:20 and 16:21	If first items are alike	File Patterns 20 and 21, respectively, before Pattern 16	19.A
	If first items are unlike	File by first different filing element in the first block	1.B
17:17	If first blocks are alike	File by first different filing element of next block	1.B
	If first blocks are unlike	File by first different filing element in the first block	1.B
17:18 and 17:19	If only the leading sections are alike	File Pattern 17 before Patterns 18 and 19, respectively	1.B

Pattern Pair	Conditions (if any)	Instructions	Applicable ALA rule Number
	If leading sections are unlike	File by first different filing element in the first block	1.B
17:20 and 17:21	If first items are alike	File Patterns 20 and 21, respectively, before Pattern 17	19.A
	If first items are unlike	File by first different filing element in the first block	1.B
18:18	If first blocks are alike	File by first different filing element of next block	1.B
	If only the leading sections are alike	File by first different filing element in the second section	1.B
	If leading sections are unlike	File by first different filing element in the first block	1.B
18:19	If only the leading sections are alike	File Pattern 19 before Pattern 18	32.C

Pattern Pair	Conditions (if any)	Instructions	Applicable ALA rule Number
	If leading sections are unlike	File by first different filing element in the first block	1.B
18:20 and 18:21	If first items are alike	File Patterns 20 and 21, respectively, before Pattern 18	19.A
	If first items are unlike	File by first different filing element in the first block	1.B
19:19	If first blocks are alike	File by first different filing element of next block	1.B
	If chronological sections only are unlike	File by numerical rank of chronological section	32.G
	If leading sections are unlike	File by first different filing element in the first block	1.B
19:20 and 19:21	If only the leading sections are alike	File Patterns 20 and 21, respectively, before Pattern 19	19.A

Pattern Pair	Conditions (if any)	Instructions	Applicable ALA rule Number
	If leading sections are unlike	File by first different filing element in the first block	1.B
20:20	If first blocks are alike	File by first different filing element of next block	32.B
	If chronological sections only are unlike	File by numerical rank of chronological section	32.G
	If only the leading sections are alike	File by first different filing element in the given name section	19.A.1)
	If leading sections are unlike	File by first different filing element in the first block	1.B
20:21	If leading sections, given name sections, and chronological sections are alike	File by first different filing element in the title	1.B
	If chronological sections only are unlike	File by numerical rank of chronological section	32.G

Pattern Pair	Conditions (if any)	Instructions	Applicable ALA rule Number
	If only the leading sections are alike	File by first different filing element in the given name section	19.A.1)
	If leading sections are unlike	File by first different filing element in the first block	1.B
21:21	If first blocks are alike	File by first different filing element of next block	32.B
	If leading sections, given name sections, and chronological sections are alike	File by first different filing element in the title	1.B
	If only the leading sections are alike	File by first different filing element in the given name section	19.A
	If leading sections are unlike	File by first different filing element in the first block	1.B

Glossary

Abbreviation

Any shortened form of a word or phrase. Examples are the E. in James E. Smith, or the St. in St. John. Also Dept. in Dept. of Agriculture.

Acronym

A word formed from letters of successive parts of a compound term. Examples are UNESCO and Laser.

Added Entry

As defined in the *ala glossary of Library Terms*, viz. a secondary entry, any other than the main entry.

Added Entry Block

Any block above the main entry block on an added entry card.

Added Entry Card

Synonym for Added Entry.

Alphabetical Order

Name popularly given to the principle of ordering letters of the English alphabet according to their numerical rank after mapping them to the first twenty-six counting numbers.

Bibliographic Unit

A term that is more precise than the traditional term "book". A bibliographic unit is a physical volume or set of such volumes when cataloged as a unit. Thus *Shepherd's Historical Atlas* (1 volume) is a bibliographic unit. *The American Educator Encyclopedia* (14 volumes) is also a bibliographic unit. The *Anglo-American Cataloging Rules** uses the term

*Anglo-American Cataloging Rules. North American edition. Chicago, American Library Association, 1967.

"bibliographic item" for the same concept. Notice that this conflicts with the term "item" as used in the *ALA Rules*.

Block

A standard location on the catalog card in which descriptive information is typed or printed. Not to be confused with the definition given in the *ALA Glossary of Library Terms*, viz. a piece of wood. The *AACR* uses the term "paragraph" for the same concept in a slightly more limited sense.

Block Content

Collective name for what is typed or printed in each block on a catalog card. Block content varies from block position. A main entry block, for example, may contain a personal author's name, but it may also contain a corporate author's name. Or it may contain a title.

Block Function

Collective name for the purpose fulfilled by each block on a catalog card. Block function varies from block content and from block position. For example, the primary added entry block (block position) may contain a person's name (block contents) but function as subject block.

Block Position

By a strictly mechanical organization principle the blocks on a catalog card can be said to have a finite number of positions. For filing purposes, the important block positions are: Added entry, Main entry, and Subsidiary descriptive blocks.

Block Role

In filing, blocks may play one of two roles: first filing block or subsequent filing block. On a main entry card, the main entry block serves as first filing block. On an added entry card, the main entry block serves as subsequent filing block.

Book

No satisfactory definition has been written so far for this term in the context of library filing. Cf. Bibliographic Unit.

Call Number Block

Designation for one of the standard block positions on a catalog card, usually in the upper left corner.

Card

As defined in the *ALA Glossary of Library Terms*, viz. a piece of cardboard used in making a library record.

Card File

A collection of catalog cards arranged in order. A catalog.

Catalog

A card file.

Compound

Synonym for compound name as defined in the *ALA Glossary of Library Terms*, viz. a name formed from two or more proper names, often connected by a hyphen, a conjunction, or a preposition.

Contextual Rank Order

A secondary ordering principle according to which entries found to be alike in terms of a primary ordering principle are ranked according to meaning or context of words.

Date

Symbols identifying a point or period of time.

Designation

A title or appellation to distinguish a person's name.

Element

In filing, elements are the constituents or typographic symbols into which an item may be resolved.

Entry

Record of a bibliographic unit in a card file.

Filing Block

see Block Role

Filing Item

A term more precise than "word". All entries are composed of items (q. v.) but not all items are filing items. For example, the initial article in "A doll's house" is an item, but not a filing item. The book title "1984" is a filing item, but not a word.

Filing Section

For purposes of filing and subarrangement, blocks are often divided into visible or imaginary sections. No concise definition has been written so far.

First Filing Block

see Block Role

Heading

Used here in sense 2 of the definition given in the *ALA Glossary of Library Terms*, viz. the word, name, or phrase at the head of an entry.

Initial

An abbreviation consisting of the first letter of a proper name.

Item

Any element or sequence of elements (letters, numerals, or

signs) enclosed by truespaces, latentspaces, or punctuation marks.

Item Transformation

The intellectual operation of mentally translating an alphabetical item such as REVOLUTION into a range of dates for chronological filing.

Latentspace

A concept according to which a non-existing space between two letters is treated as if it existed. For example, the letters A, b, c in "Abc" are separated by latentspaces.

Letter

An alphabetical element representing a sound made by the human voice. For example, x is a letter. It represents the sound "eks". Contrast this with X, which is not a letter because it represents a numerical concept, the value 10.

Main Entry Block

One of the standard block positions on the catalog card. The top-most block in a main entry card. It is the one block that is present on all catalog cards under the unit card system. It contains the words under which the book is "entered". The *AACR* uses the term "heading" for this concept in a slightly more limited sense.

Main Entry Card

A main entry. A card that carries full cataloging information. The unit card. The main entry has no added entry blocks and is therefore recognized by the fact that the main entry block is the top-most block on the card.

Missing Symbol

An element that is not printed on the card but is mentally inserted before the item is filed. For example, the a between M and c in McGraw is a missing symbol.

Natural Title

The title of a bibliographic unit as it appears "naturally" on the title page. As opposed to the Uniform Title, q.v.

Number

Any numerical value represented by one or more numerals. Not to be confused with the definition given in the *ALA Glossary of Library Terms*, viz. an issue of a periodical.

Numeral

An element that represents a numerical value. The symbols 3 and X, for example, are numerals.

Numerical Order

One of the primary ordering principles in filing. According to this principle the historical subject subdivision "1798" files before "1812".

Prefix

An article, preposition, or contraction of either or both, that is part of a proper name, such as the "Los" of "Los Angeles" and the "Du" of "Du Barry".

Primary Added Entry Block

In an added entry, the top-most block on the card.

Pseudo-Item

Any item in an entry that is disregarded in filing. The "the" of "The way of all flesh", when that title occupies the primary added entry block, is a pseudo-item.

Pseudo-Letter

An element that looks like a letter but is not. The Roman numeral M, for example, is a pseudo-letter. So is the second u in humour.

Pseudo-Position

The imaginary position that certain numerical items are assumed to occupy. Thus "7th Army" is mentally re-arranged to "Army Number 7" before filing. This moves the numerical designation from a frontal to a dorsal position.

Pseudospace

A space between two elements that is considered non-existent for filing purposes, causing two items to be treated as one. Thus, the space between e and F in De Funiak Springs is a pseudospace.

Punctuation Mark

A typographic symbol conventionally used to indicate the end of a sentence or phrase, such as the period, the comma, or the dash. Hyphens and apostrophes are not considered punctuation marks.

Range of Dates

A method of indicating a defined time period that employs two numbers, such as "1914-1918".

Rank

Key principle in filing. Two entries can be filed only if they differ in rank.

Rank Order

A theoretical principle according to which entries are placed in sequence in a file. Rank order may be determined on a numerical or on a logical basis.

Record

Synonymous with entry. A card or decklet of cards on which a description of the cataloged book is "recorded".

Section

Two or more items in a block separated by punctuation marks. Not to be confused with the definition given in the *ALA Glossary of Library Terms*, viz. part of a book case, newspaper, or other physical ensemble. The *AACR*, revised chapter 6, uses the term "area" for a similar concept.

Sign

A typographic symbol other than a letter, a numeral, or a punctuation mark. Examples are $ and %.

Source Entry

A functional name for an entry that is to be filed into a catalog or target file.

Space

A gap between two elements that is wider than the small space that is left when two symbols are printed next to each other.

Subarrange

When two entries have been found to be of equal rank in the first compared section or block, subarrangement is made by a subsequent section or block.

Subject Block

A functional name for an added entry block that contains a subject heading.

Subject Heading

As defined in the *ALA Glossary of Library Terms*, viz. a word or group of words indicating a subject under which all material dealing with the same theme is entered in a catalog.

Subsequent Filing Block

A block that is considered only in subarrangement.

Subsidiary Descriptive Block

Any one of the several possible descriptive blocks on a card that follow the main entry block.

Symbol Translation

The process of mentally converting unmappable typographic symbols so that they may be ranked. Thus, 2 is translated to Two and filed alphabetically.

Target Entry

A functional name for an entry in a catalog or target file.

Target File

A functional name for a card file or catalog.

Tracings Block

Used synonymously with the term "tracing" as defined in the *ALA Glossary of Library Terms*, viz. the record on the main entry card of all the additional headings under which the work is represented in the catalog.

Truespace

A space between two elements that is regarded as a space for filing purposes.

Typographic Section

Any item or group of items bordered on one or both sides by punctuation marks.

Typographic Symbol

An element; one of the constituents into which items can be analysed. Any piece of type in the printer's font. Letters are typographic symbols, but not all typographic symbols are letters.

Uniform Title

As defined in the *ALA Glossary of Library Terms*, viz. the distinctive title by which a work which has appeared under varying titles and in various versions is most generally known.

Word

See Item.

Index

ALA Rules not suitable for automation, 99
ALA Rules weak on general principles, 7
Abbreviations, 67
Added entry blocks, 28
Added entry card, 33
Alphabetical filing, seen as a special case of numerical filing, 73
Apostrophe, ignored in filing, 68
Author blocks, 31
Automation requires full understanding of filing process, 12, 99

Basic principle of filing catalog cards, 19
Block content, 29
Block function, 31
Block layout of a catalog card, simple schematic, 25; full schematic, 28
Block position, 28
Block roles, 32

Call number block, 28
Card layout, 24-34
Chronological subject subdivisions, 76
Collation block, 29
Compounds, 66
Contextual rank order, 77

Dates after names, 58

Decision flow chart, 84-88; examples, 89-98
Designations of rank or status, 57; of relationship between author and work, 71

Element, 62
Entry, concept, 15; flagged for machine filing, 102
Equivalent heading, 23
Equivalent names, 23

Filing, defined, 15; basic principle, 19
Filing section, 55
First filing block, 32
First filing blocks identical in two compared cards, 44

Item, definition with examples, 66
Item transformation for numerical items, 82; for alphabetical items, 79

Kind of entry, 10

Latentspace, 63
Letters, 65

Machine filing, examples, 103
Main entry block, schematic, 28; role, 34; content, 29-30; function, 32
Main entry card, 32